Listen,
God Is Speaking
to You

TRUE STORIES OF
HIS LOVE AND GUIDANCE

Quin Sherrer

SERVANT PUBLICATIONS
ANN ARBOR, MICHIGAN

Vine Books is an imprint of Servant Publications especially designed to serve evangelical Christians.

All Scripture quotations, unless otherwise indicated, are taken from the HOLY BIBLE, NEW INTERNATIONAL VERSION, © 1973, 1978, 1984 by International Bible Society. Used by permission of Zondervan Publishing House. All rights reserved. Other versions are abbreviated as follows: AMPLI-FIED (The Amplified Bible), NAS (New American Standard), NKJV (New King James Version), KJV (King James Version).

Some names and locations have been changed throughout the book to protect privacy.

Published by Servant Publications
P.O. Box 8617
Ann Arbor, Michigan 48107

Cover design: The Office of Bill Chiaravalle, Sisters, Oregon
Cover photograph: Graphistock

Printed in the United States of America
ISBN 0-7394-0586-1

Contents

Foreword

Intimidating, that's what it is. Being asked to write a foreword for one of Quin Sherrer's books is like asking a six-year-old Little Leaguer to give an endorsement for Mark McGuire. (For all you baseball illiterates, he's the new home run king, having shattered the records of both Babe Ruth and Roger Maris.) For us wannabe writers, Quin Sherrer is a standard bearer. We're learning; she's a teacher. We do some writing, she's a writer. Big difference!

Not only is it intimidating, however. It is also a tremendous honor. When you hold someone in the place of esteem in which I hold Quin, the honor of being asked to do this is profound. "Thanks, Quin, you made my day."

What topic could possibly deserve more of our attention than listening to God? When the source of all life and wisdom speaks, those who would be wise listen. The foolish either don't care to or don't learn how. The fruit of both is the same: destructive ignorance.

This book is for those who would be wise ... those who believe God speaks and who desire to hear Him. It is also for those who *want* to believe He speaks, but aren't sure; for after reading it, your hope will be satisfied, your fears allayed: God does, indeed, still speak today.

And what happens when He speaks to us? The literal Greek rendering of Luke 1:37 is, "For no word spoken by God is without power." The context of the verse is Mary's conception of Christ. She was being told, "It will happen, Mary, because I have declared it, and My words have power to perform or create." For us, as well, when God speaks there is power in His words: to change us, equip us, empower us, mature us, save us, heal us, prepare us—the list could continue. Indeed, the very key to life is listening to God: "Man shall not live by bread alone, but by every word that proceeds from the mouth of God."

When God speaks, worlds become.
When God speaks, storms cease.
When God speaks, mountains shake.
When God speaks, heaven and hell stand at attention.
When God speaks, nations rise and fall.

And when God speaks to people, lives are changed. Like the Samaritans in John 4, who said, "We had heard about you and it was great, but now we've heard you ourselves and we will never be the same" (Sheets' paraphrase), this book will help you listen to God and you will never be the same!

With artistic skill, using real life stories as the paint and the ways and word of God as the brush, Quin gives us more than words—she gives us a painting. Some, like Quin, simply have that rare ability to paint with words. Sentences become images, paragraphs become scenes. She's one of the authors who, when reading, I find myself thinking, "I wish I had said that!"

And I think her propensity toward using so many true life stories is what makes it all so intensely practical and easy to understand. Some people can make truth so boring and complicated! To the contrary, you'll find this, and all of Quin's books, hard to put down. I'm sorry, but this is a "read till 2 A.M., lose some sleep" kind of book. It is filled with wisdom, tackling the difficult questions and issues of life which so few will touch. After reading it, you'll agree that Quin does this with depth, sensitivity, and rare insight.

This book will draw you closer to the Father, which should be the litmus test of any Christian book, and enable you to help others do the same. When facing life's obstacles you will trust Him more, even when you don't fully understand—especially when you don't understand. You will pray more and prosper more. You'll walk through the sometimes "jungle" of life without stepping into the hidden pits of quicksand as you learn to *Listen*, for *God Is Speaking to You.*

Dutch Sheets
Colorado Springs, Colorado

Acknowledgments

I want to express my appreciation and thanks to three special editors who have been my cheerleaders and friends for many years:

Beth Feia, Ann Spangler, and Gwen Ellis.

I also wish to pay tribute with a heart full of gratitude to three devoted men of God who have helped me learn to hear God's voice more clearly over the years as they have spoken into my life. My special thanks to each of you:

Pastor Peter Lord
Park Avenue Baptist Church, Titusville, Florida

The Reverend Forrest Mobley
Saint Andrew's Episcopal Church, Destin, Florida

Pastor Dutch Sheets
Springs Harvest Fellowship, Colorado Springs, Colorado.

And to all my faithful intercessors, another big thank-you. May God Himself reward you!

Dedication

God brings people of His choice into our lives for His purpose. The Reverend Forrest Mobley has been one of those special people in my life, although, in the nearly thirty years we've known each other, our friendship has grown mostly by long-distance communication.

I'll never forget that Thursday night renewal service at his church, St. Andrew's Episcopal, when I was visiting my mom, who had retired to Destin, Florida. He was her pastor. But he'd never met me.

After the service, I asked him to pray for me. He bowed his head in silent prayer, then he said rather boldly, "I'm sorry, but I can't. God shows me there is someone you need to forgive before I pray."

I was in shock. Here was a pastor who knew literally nothing about me, yet God had showed him I still had unforgiveness in my heart—toward my dad. After Forrest shared Scriptures with me, showing me why I must forgive, I spoke my forgiveness aloud. That night on my knees in his office, I ended up asking Jesus to be my *Lord*, not just my Savior.

From then on, whenever I visited Mom, I'd head for St. Andrew's, where services were held each morning. Afterward, Forrest might stop to talk. One day, he suggested I write up the story of a doctor in his church who had been healed of leukemia. He laid his hands on me and prayed for a new anointing of the Holy Spirit for the task. I wrote the article and entered it in the *Guideposts* magazine writers' contest. It won me a week of training in New York under some top Christian editors.

Forrest would sometimes invite me to ride with him as he made pastoral and hospital visits. All along the way he discipled me in very practical ways of the Lord. I especially enjoyed watching him serve the Eucharist to shut-ins, most of whom couldn't get to church for Communion.

One night I was tossing in my bed—450 miles from Destin— because my doctor had called to say I had a serious breast lump problem and he wanted to operate as soon as possible. At that moment, God told Forrest to call me and pray for me—though he had no way of knowing my physical need. After I told him about it, he prayed for my healing and God touched me. Tests later proved that I had been healed.

Once when I was betrayed by a close friend and was crying my eyes out, Forrest reminded me that Jesus forgave His betrayer friend named Judas and I could too.

He even came the long distance to help LeRoy and me dedicate our home to Christ.

Forrest always talked about Jesus as though He was right there with us. He drew me and all others who knew him closer and closer to our Savior. He went on to get his doctorate, serve as dean of a cathedral, and head up a counseling center. But to me he is just Forrest—a pastor who still phones occasionally to ask what God is doing in my life. He has dared to be honest with me, faithful to pray, and has always encouraged me to stretch into areas of ministry I didn't even know would be possible.

Thank you, Forrest, you who know how to hear clearly from God, for opening up the Scriptures and teaching me in practical ways how I too can hear Him more clearly.

Introduction

The voice of the Lord is over the waters;
the God of glory thunders....
The voice of the Lord is powerful;
the voice of the Lord is majestic....
The voice of the Lord strikes
with flashes of lightening.
The voice of the Lord shakes the desert....
And in his temple all cry, "Glory!"

PSALM 29:3a, 4, 7-8a, 9b

Since ancient times no one has heard, no ear has perceived, no eye has seen any God besides you, who acts on behalf of those who wait for him.

ISAIAH 64:4

This book is a collection of true stories that illustrate how God has spoken and guided people like you and me in our generation. It is my hope that we will get a broader view of the myriad ways God speaks to us. Sometimes very gently, quietly, and simply. Other times rather dramatically and forcefully.

These stories graphically illustrate how individuals faced situations that taught them how to seek God fervently. Though many struggled, they looked to God through trying times. And as you'll see, God worked in their lives. Together we will learn how to:

- look for God in unexpected places
- discern what is and what is not His voice
- be patient while waiting on the Lord
- be quiet and listen expectantly
- believe He wants to speak
- surrender our self-will so God can get through to us
- let go of fear and obey His promptings
- become more able to be guided by God through practice.

These goals have one purpose that is at the heart of all that God does: He wants us to be totally dependent on Him and have intimate communication with Him—not just during our private devotional time, but all the time!

It is my prayer you will be encouraged to depend on God more wholeheartedly and listen more intently for His guidance, even in the nitty-gritty aspects of your life.

Quin Sherrer
Colorado Springs

PART 1

How Does God Speak?

֍

[Jesus said,] I will ask the Father, and He will give you another Comforter (Counselor, Helper, Intercessor, Advocate, Strengthener, and Standby), that He may remain with you forever—The Spirit of Truth.... He will teach you all things.

JOHN 14:16-17a, 26b AMPLIFIED

Give much quality time to communion with the Holy Spirit. He will not speak to anyone who is in a hurry. All of God's Word is about waiting on Him! ... Wait patiently. Seek the Lord and minister praises to Him. Take authority over every other voice that whispers thoughts to you. Believe that the Spirit is greater than these, and that He will not let you be deceived or blind. Be willing to set your heart on Him.

David Wilkerson[1]

Most of us, if we are honest, have a longing to hear God speak to us—directly and very personally. We want our prayers answered and our lives touched by His hand. We desire His guidance and His protection. We want Him to reveal the mysteries of our lives and to use us to touch others. Will He speak? Can we hear?

Maybe we think that He will not speak to little people like us. Or perhaps we have too narrow a view of how He speaks today. Maybe we've thought that, unless we hear some roaring voice from the sky, God hasn't spoken. We tend to box Him in by our limited expectations. When the signs we hope for don't come, we feel He is not listening or that He does not care.

But the truth is that God is always trying to speak to us. He wants to speak to us more than we want to hear Him. When we let go of our preconceived notions of how He speaks, when He speaks, and to whom He speaks and simply start to listen anew with childlike faith, we'll be surprised at how readily we can hear Him.

He is with us at every turn. He uses everything and anything to call us to Himself.

The Holy Spirit's Assignment

Instead of a direct, audible voice, thundering from heaven, God's Holy Spirit often speaks into our hearts. The Holy Spirit not only speaks, He guides us. He reveals the things of God, strengthens and encourages us, convicts us of sin, and loves through us. He also helps us pray.[2]

Mark Virkler wrote:

The voice of God, I've discovered, is Spirit-to-spirit communication, the Holy Spirit speaking directly to my spirit. It is sensed as a spontaneous thought, idea, word, feeling or vision. Thoughts from my mind, on the other hand, are analytical and cognitive. I reason them out. Thoughts from my heart are spontaneous.... I am not saying that every spontaneous thought is the Holy Spirit speaking to us. I am saying that spontaneity is heart-level communication.[3]

God Even Cares About Christmas Gifts

A businessman named Scott took a request to God. In turn God spoke to him in a way he couldn't have dreamed. He was new to the things of God, but when he heard His inner voice, he recognized it and obeyed.

What could Scott give his three employees for Christmas? He'd pondered this question for several weeks. The year had been a financially lean one. He didn't have any money to spend on gifts. Yet his heart yearned to honor them in some way. These three—a young male college student, an African-American retiree, and one woman—had worked long hours beside him to make his new business go. In the process they'd also become his friends.

"Give them the gift of yourself," the Lord seemed to whisper one day as he was leaving his store.

"How? What?" Scott asked, puzzled. Then the idea popped into his head, straight from heaven. Jesus Himself had done it for His beloved disciples. "Yes, Lord," he replied. "I'll do it."

That Christmas Eve, he shut the door to his business earlier than usual and asked the three to sit in special chairs he'd set out.

Taking a basin of water and a towel, he washed their feet. As he did, his tears spilled down into the basin. Then, while he dried their feet, he told each one how much he appreciated his or her efforts for him that year. He asked God to reward them for their faithfulness and friendship.

Each of them went home with a heartfelt gift of love, given by someone who had heard the Lord speak and was willing to obey. Late that evening the African-American called Scott at home. "I can't believe what I experienced today. It brought me to another level of knowing God's love—kneeling at my feet and washing them. Your kindness touched me more than you will ever know. God bless you, and Merry Christmas."

Scott sought God on a small matter, God gave him an idea, and then God used His Word to put "flesh" on the idea. The gift was powerful and much more effective than any material gift. This is often God's way. Scott could have looked for God to give him money—something obvious—and only expected that, but he didn't put God in a box.

Amazing, isn't it? God actually speaks to us in the everyday parts of our lives.

Learning to Discern His Voice

Right now you may be saying, "Yes, but how do I know the voice I hear is really God's talking to me?" There are always three possibilities when you "hear" a voice:

1. It could be God speaking through the Holy Spirit. You will know because whatever is spoken will be consistent with God's character and His Word.

2. It could be a demonic voice representing Satan. Sometimes you'll know because the thought is not motivated by love and humility or it is centered in condemnation. Be aware: the enemy is a crafty deceiver.

3. It could be your own inner voice "speaking" a thought based on your logical reasoning, your will, or your self-centered emotions.

If you have difficulty discerning which voice it might be, you may want to say a prayer like this: "Lord, I desire to hear Your voice and be led by You. If this is Your Holy Spirit speaking, please cause this impression I have to become more clear and urgent. If you want me to take any action, cause the urge to do this thing to increase. If this impression I have is not of you, please cause it to fade.

"By the authority of the blood of Jesus that covers me, I address any evil spirits present and command them to be silent in Jesus' name. I will listen only to the voice of my Shepherd. Thank you, Father, for speaking to me by whatever means You choose as I wait upon You. I promise to obey that which You speak. Amen."[4]

Other Ways He Speaks

God can speak to us through other means as well:

- an "internal witness" or a "knowing" in our innermost being, a settling peace, a conviction that the decision we might normally fret over is the right one. For instance, a woman decides to take a job that pays less money but has less stress than the better-paying one. She experiences peace after praying about her decision, though she'll earn less money. She just knows this is the right decision for her at this time.

- a supernatural witness, such as visions, dreams, miracles, or a prophetic voice. Be open. Look and listen. What if someone has a "word" from God that you are going to a Third World nation to speak to their political leaders? Too bizarre, you may think. But this happened to a friend of mine, who sensed that this was a legitimate message from God. Responding to this call, she traveled to that nation not once but twice within a year and had an effective audience with their leaders by a door God opened for her.

- circumstances, such as closed or open doors or a serendipi-tous meeting that brings us an opportunity.

God speaks in these and many other ways. If we are open to hearing His voice at every turn, we will begin to recognize it with much greater frequency.

How Can We Learn To Hear?

When we really want to know someone well, don't we spend time with him or her? We listen, ask for an opinion, observe reactions. In the same way, we get to know God better by spending time with Him, becoming actively involved in the process.

1. We begin to develop a relationship with God—an intimate friendship where we bring all of our concerns to Him. We get to know who He is and how He works. Reading and studying the Bible are critical, since these are primary means He uses to speak to us about who He is and how He wants us to live.

2. As we grow in understanding of who God is, we learn to become discerning, distinguishing His voice in the midst of all the other voices around us.

3. We grow in confidence that we will recognize His voice at every turn in each moment of need.

Does the Voice Gently Lead You?

My friend Elizabeth Alves, who has taught thousands how to discern God's voice, says:

> One test to determine whether you are hearing the Holy Spirit is to ask: Is the voice gently leading, or is it commanding and harsh? God's voice gently guides and encourages, giving hope (see Psalm 18:35; Isaiah 40:11; James 3:17). God leads; Satan drives (John 10:4). God convicts; Satan condemns and brings guilt (Psalm 8:12). God woos; Satan tugs hard. When God speaks, He does not use fear to motivate. If fear overcomes you, it is the enemy speaking, not God (See 2 Timothy 1:7).[5]

God may even speak to us in pictures in our minds. I've known some people who see messages run like a ticker tape in their minds when God is speaking to them. Have you ever received a God-inspired thought for your business? You soon realized it was not your own bright idea. Or have you had someone's name suddenly pop into your thoughts? After a while you finally figure out that God is trying to get you to pray for her. Later you learn she was in dire need of direction at the moment you prayed.

Most often, God's Spirit speaks to us in what's been called His "still small voice." But we have to learn to recognize His voice. Become familiar with it. My former pastor, Peter Lord, taught us to begin to hear from God by asking Him simple questions. He'd suggest, "Ask God what He thinks of you. Get off alone and write down the impressions you get." This is a good place to start. You will hear Him tell you, no doubt, how much He loves and treasures you.

Other Quiet Time Guidelines

Author Elizabeth Alves gives further guidelines to hearing the voice of God. They work best during a time of sitting quietly before Him, she suggests. "Bind the voice of the enemy before you start to pray. Do this in the name of Jesus." To some Christians, this means to restrain Satan's demonic forces by addressing them directly.

Then trust the Holy Spirit. He will lead you and guide you into all truth. Submit your own will and reasoning to the Holy Spirit. Then give Him your undivided attention. Often it helps to read God's Word as you sit. Then with a note-book close by, you might write down what the Spirit of the Lord may speak—even impressions or pictures.

The Holy Spirit sometimes speaks through music. So you may want to sit in the Lord's presence listening to praise music. Other times the Holy Spirit wants us to just worship the Lord. And don't be afraid of silence.[6]

We must learn the discipline of quietly waiting and listening. Each of us can hear from God, be discerning, and be led by the Holy Spirit.

She Almost Missed God's Direction

Just one passage of Scripture, when it penetrates your heart, can change your whole life.

Babs was a certified public accountant and taught accounting at the University of Texas. One day she got a phone call asking her to move to San Antonio to work for an evangelist.

"I was not interested," she recalls. "I had a good job. I loved where I lived. But as I hung up the phone and walked into the den, the Spirit of the Lord spoke to me through a Scripture I'd memorized earlier: 'Behold, ... new things do I declare: before they spring forth I tell you of them' (Is 42:9, KJV). The phrase 'new things ... I tell you' was emphatic to me. So I knew I'd better reconsider. I ended up going. As a result, I met the man who became my husband."

When She Didn't Obey God's Prompting

Sometimes we don't obey God's whisper and we suffer the consequences. This is true even in small decisions we make. Iloa has frequent pain that reminds her of the time she didn't heed God's voice.

I was hurrying to leave the house for my teaching job—fifth and sixth graders. My teacher husband, our two daughters, and two neighbor girls were already in the car, waiting for me. I was about to put on a pair of heels that matched my outfit when I sensed an inner voice say, *"Wear flats, not heels."*

I disregarded the voice. "It must be my imagination," I thought. I slipped into high heels. As I was rushing out the back door, the heel of my left shoe caught on the top step. I felt something in my leg twist and snap. I landed on the sidewalk at the bottom of the steps.

X rays revealed a chunk of bone had separated near my ankle. The next day I had surgery to put two steel pins in the bone. For the next two months I was confined at home in a cast. Of course, during those months of recuperation, I acknowledged that the voice I had heard was God warning me not to wear those shoes. My pride had gotten in the way. Now I listen more carefully when He speaks, and I don't wave it away as though it's my imagination.

God Taught Her Contentment

Jessie, who was widowed at age twenty-three with two young girls to raise, was lonely. One night, when she told God how unhappy she was, she heard Him reply, *"You don't have to be happy, but you can be content."*

"That did it!" she says. "From that day, I asked the Lord to work contentment in me. And through the years when things would upset me, God gave me the contentment I needed to get through whatever situation I was in."

Jessie, who had often prayed for another husband, changed her prayer: "God, I am content. If it is your plan for me to marry, you can bring a man into my life; if not, I won't ask again." And she didn't. After seventeen years of widowhood, God sent Addison as a gift to her—as her husband.[7]

As God's children, we can ask Him to speak in every situation we face.

Developing a Discerning Ear

Peter Lord tells the story of a young man who came to his home for a wedding reception. The pastor noticed the young man peering intently at the plants beside his walkway and asked him why.

"There are eighteen different kinds of crickets in these bushes," he said.

Although Pastor Lord had lived in that house for years, he had never consciously heard a cricket. However, the visitor was a graduate student in entomology at the University of Florida. He had learned to distinguish over two hundred different types of cricket calls with his natural ear in order to earn his doctorate.[8]

Oh, that we could be as familiar with the voice of God. Jesus strongly emphasized our need to listen. At least fifteen times He says, "He that hath ears to hear, let him hear" (Mt 11:15, KJV).

When I was a youngster, we lived in a boarding house right beside the railroad tracks. When we first moved there I woke up every night at the sound of the shrill whistle blowing as the train passed by. But after a few months, I got so accustomed to it, I never even heard it. I just slept soundly. My ears were dull to its alarm.

A lot of Christians are like that. When we first accept the Lord, we are excited. The God of the universe is our friend. We are astounded that He guides us and speaks to us. But our temptation over time is to grow complacent and begin to let other voices crowd out God's. We lose our childlike faith, that eager expectation of God's action in our life. We become insensitive to the Holy Spirit, our teacher.

Why Doesn't God Boom His Voice?

As I was about to slip into a hot tub of water to relax before the next seminar meeting, the hotel's fire alarm went off. Then a booming voice came over the intercom: "We have an emergency. Go to the nearest stairs. Do not use the elevator. Leave the building immediately. Evacuate!" The noise was deafening. I threw on my clothes and started to run.

"Sometimes I wish God's voice would boom that loud when He needs to warn me, to get my attention," I thought to myself as I flew down the seven flights of stairs, panting until I reached the front lawn and the sight of a red fire engine.

Why doesn't He speak like that? Perhaps because then I would not be required to seek Him, to express my desire for Him. God wants us to want Him and desires a personal relationship based on love and trust. He respects our wills, so He doesn't hit us over the head. Rather, He chooses to let us find Him when we wholeheartedly seek Him.

God cares about every aspect of our lives. He desires to express His love and nearness to us. He longs to guide us. He seeks to strengthen us for life's challenges. He enables us to serve others and pray for them. He is eager to comfort and to sustain us. He communicates with us even in our dreams. He speaks protection into our lives.

This book describes God in action, speaking at every turn in the lives of people like you and me. You'll learn that God can speak anytime, anywhere, anyhow.

Are we listening?

Prayer

Lord, thank You that You still yearn to speak to us today. You can speak in a still small voice, through a Bible passage, through a friend, or through a thought You drop into my mind. Lord, give me discernment to know which is Your voice, which is my own, and which is the voice of the enemy. I need discernment. Let the Holy Spirit teach me. I ask this in Jesus' name. Amen.

PART 2

His Voice at Life's Crossroads

&

Therefore consider carefully how you listen....

LUKE 8:18a

A basic principle of spiritual discernment and guidance is that we are seeking the best for today, for this time and place, for this point in our pilgrimage. God leads us one step at a time. We may wish that God would map out the next few years or even our whole life for us. Some Christians are stymied in decision-making because they demand that all their questions be answered, with all the implications of a decision clearly delineated....

But this long-term knowledge is not granted to us. We cannot see beyond the immediate future.

Gordon T. Smith[1]

"Where do I go from here, God? I don't know what to do."

One of the most critical times in which we need to hear from God is when we must make crucial decisions. An opportunity may be before us or we may find ourselves in a hard place where we are really stuck. We need God to give us a sense of what to do at the crossroads we encounter.

Whether it's a move, a job, a troubling relationship, or a child in crisis, we long for God's direction. Sometimes there are circumstances in life over which we have no control—and we feel ourselves spinning downward. *Help, Lord.*

In times of decisions we can become vulnerable, afraid, uncertain, confused, even angry. God wants to speak to us and help us move forward wisely and confidently. Are we attuned to hear Him?

When a Teenager Is Pregnant

Often the most heart-wrenching times of decision come when a child is in trouble. Helen faced circumstances out of her control that sent her into a tailspin when her teenage daughter Lisa admitted she was pregnant. Helen experienced every negative emotion imaginable.

As a single mother herself, she had such high hopes for her brilliant daughter. She had a decision to make. Would she wallow in her depression and anger? Or would she forgive and move forward? She described her feelings:

I was angry with Lisa, but I really wanted to hurt Kenny. He is a few years older than Lisa and I felt he took advantage of an inexperienced teenager. I wanted to punch him in the stomach, stomp his toes, and generally beat him up.

I was devastated and filled with shame, as it seemed my best efforts at child rearing had failed. With a dark cloud now hanging over Lisa's promising future, I felt disappointed, angry, hurt, grieved by this news. Then I entered a three-month period of depression. Although I never turned my back on God, I felt numb and lifeless, not caring about anything anymore.

One day, almost three months after Lisa's announcement, I was sitting alone at the kitchen table. In the Spirit, I felt and saw the Lord come into the room. Like a good friend would do, He gently tapped me on the shoulder and said reassuringly, *"Don't you think My love is big enough to cover this situation?"*

That moment was the turning point for me in this journey. I suddenly saw the whole problem from God's perspective—that with Him it wasn't hopeless. Now I could accept Lisa more freely. I repented for my anger, forgave both of them for disappointing me, and moved out of the holding pattern to get on with my life.[2]

Lisa had barely finished her second year of college when she gave birth to a healthy little boy. Today she is raising her son and about to graduate. It isn't easy being a single mom, but she is making it. God is at work in her life as she calls out to Him, bringing good out of an imperfect situation.

Her Message Came Through a Friend

Sometimes we feel we must save certain people in our lives—whether siblings, spouses, friends, coworkers, or children. We feel compelled to cushion them from life's harsh realities or rescue them from the consequences of their choices. God wants us to learn to let go of responsibilities that are too big for us, to allow Him to work, to allow Him to be their Savior.

Pam had to make that decision when her son Mark came back to live at home after a history of drug abuse. Pam was beside herself. He would not work. He would not come home at night when his mother and stepfather asked him to. No amount of coaxing, warning, or loving seemed to reach him.

One day as Pam prayed, she asked, "God, what do I do? If I make him move out, he may go back on drugs in no time. Please show me the right thing to do. Please speak to me."

Just a few minutes after she'd prayed, the phone rang. A friend from her church whom she trusted told her, "Pam, for a while now I have known something God wanted you to know, but at the right time. Today He told me to call you. By allowing Mark to stay you are allowing a spirit of rebellion to run through your home. Our homes are to be places of peace. Yours is not. If you don't do something about Mark—and make some hard choices—his rebellion will soon move onto his younger brother."

Pam thanked him and began to ponder his words. Yes, if he leaves home he might return to the drug scene, but she believed she had heard God's voice through her friend. She drove to town, found an apartment, and paid one month's rent. That night she told Mark he was going to move. He didn't like the news one bit.

Pam remained strong and stern. In the course of talking with his friends, she found out he was already back on drugs and had been abusing them while in her home. Learning this only reaffirmed her resolve.

When he moved out, he did go downhill quickly, she remembers. She was miserable watching his descent. It brought him to a place of no hope, and he hit rock bottom. Finally, Mark consented to counseling, became drug-free, and enlisted in the Army. Today he is a fine young man and Pam is very proud of him. She often looks back to that crucial day when her friend called, encouraging her to take action she knew all along she should do but needed reassurance. Her tough love allowed God to work.

To Move or Not to Move

We all will face decisions that affect our family life, our finances, our physical comforts. Most of these challenge us to be willing to move into the unknown and out of our comfort zone. At such times of decision, we may find ourselves more earnestly looking to God for His direction. And He does speak.

Sometimes during these crossroads times, we not only seek God's answer but also ask others to pray with us to help us hear God. That's what happened to my husband, LeRoy, and me concerning an important decision.

"Look, I can retire in two weeks," LeRoy announced, as he came in the kitchen door that late November afternoon. He handed me a letter he'd gotten that morning at the Kennedy Space Center, where he was an aeronautical engineer.

"What? You are barely fifty. How can that be?" I asked.

"Well, it's something new. Seems that since I have worked at least twenty years for the government and have reached fifty, I have the option of taking an early retirement. I have to decide in two weeks. What do you think? It will certainly mean much less retirement money than if we wait until I'm sixty-two."

"Two weeks to decide?" I questioned. "Wow. This will need lots of thought and prayer."

We'd never suspected he'd leave the space center until we had no more college bills and were really retirement age—you know, gray hair and all. We still had three kids to get through college—the oldest had just finished her sophomore year. But LeRoy was having back problems and his future health was uncertain.

We had two primary geographic options. We could stay where we lived—in a church we loved, with lots of friends, in a town where our children had grown up. Or we could move up to northwest Florida, where we had five acres in the piney woods near Destin, some fifteen miles from my mother.

We asked our pastor, Peter Lord, and our home Bible group to seek the Lord with us for an answer. In the meantime, the more LeRoy and I prayed about it, the more we sensed it was God's blessing for him to take early retirement. Yet we faced the fact that we had little savings for our expenses now, let alone the future. God was asking us to trust Him for the needed income to get our children through college.

Decision one was made. Yes, retire. But were we to leave familiar ground for unfamiliar?

Pastor Lord prayed with us. Finally, one night he told us frankly, "I sensed God is saying that you can retire, but I am not clear on whether you are to stay or move. Naturally, I'd want you to stay. Our church needs you."

I wrote many prayer entries in my journal in those next few days. Then LeRoy and I both felt we were to move closer to my mom. He signed his retirement papers and attended a party in his honor just before Christmas. Now came the task of selling our home. "How much?" I asked God as I reflected on the many happy memories of family life in this wonderful twelve-year-old two-story house.

I wrote in my prayer journal the amount God impressed on my mind to ask for the sale of the house. Christmas came and went. I believed God had told me that by the end of March we'd be moved. Our youngest child moved in with her grand-mother and enrolled in high school in the area where we'd be living. Our other two returned to college.

One Sunday morning Rudy dropped by for coffee before church. Though he'd been in our home every Sunday night for six years as a member of our Bible study group, he had never had a tour of the whole house.

"Why don't you buy our house, Rudy?" I asked, wondering afterward what made me so bold. I knew he'd thought for a long time of moving to our town because he had a long com-mute to our church. "Let me show you through the upstairs. It would sleep your family well."

He liked it. So did his wife. They bought our house for the exact amount I had written in my prayer journal—and in March we moved our belongings 450 miles north. We rented a house in the same block where my mom lived.

Within a year, LeRoy's back condition improved. We used the money from the sale of our house to build a house on our property in the woods. Soon we knew why we'd moved. The Lord had prompted our relocation because He knew Mom would need us nearby as she fought cancer. We were there to help her as best we could during her last days.

LeRoy worked for a local contractor until we got all our children through college and then through Bible school. Finally, he said it was his turn to go to a Bible college, in Dallas. After he graduated from there, again we had to decide where to live. We visited the Kennedy Space Center area, where Pastor Lord prayed with us again, asking God if we were to return. He assured us we could be used in the church's increased outreach if we did.

What a hard choice for me. My heart wanted to go there; I was a native Floridian. But Dutch Sheets, a pastor in Colorado whom we had known while LeRoy was in Bible college, also invited us to come be a part of his new and growing church.

Bathing our decision in prayer—and asking many others to pray with us—we finally made the most unlikely choice (in purely human terms) to move to Colorado Springs.

Again, I soon knew it was the right decision! Pastor Dutch was a wonderful support to me during the years I served on the board of directors for Women's Aglow Fellowship at the national and international levels. In fact, he became one of our Aglow national advisors. He is still faithful to cover me in prayer whenever I travel to speak. I've considered it a privilege to sit under this anointed Bible scholar—now very well known since the publication of his book, *Intercessory Prayer*.

Today LeRoy, at an age when most of his former coworkers are enjoying retirement, is an associate pastor under Pastor Dutch, visiting the sick, assisting with cell groups, and overseeing the food pantry.

God's ways are always higher and better than ours. I've learned that being open to His nudges into the unknown can yield great riches and blessings.

Asking, Fasting, Waiting

Just as LeRoy and I had to wait on the Lord, so did Emma.

Unexpectedly jobless on returning to the United States from China following the Tiananmen Square massacre, I didn't know what to do. So I visited friends and family in various states and finally went to stay with relatives in New England.

At first all was well. However, with each passing day some family tensions began to gnaw at me. I wanted to leave but could find no place to go. I wanted a job but only found work as a substitute teacher. I wanted a solution, but heaven seemed silent.

Finally, I drove to a nearby mountain to spend the day seeking the Lord through fasting and prayer. Toward sunset I heard an inner voice promising, *"I'll act in two weeks. Go back. Say nothing and wait."* Peace and certainty filled me as I returned to my room to wait and see what the Lord would do.

Exactly two weeks later an acquaintance phoned from Hong Kong. "My school in Canton just lost an English teacher. Could you come immediately?"

I prayed. Family and friends prayed. God gave each of us the same answer: "Go!" Arrangements easily fell in place. In less than three weeks I was again in China teaching English.

Where to Live?

In Emma's case, God spoke through an open door, but often He chooses to lead us by speaking through His Word. The Bible can confirm, encourage, convict, challenge, or direct us.

When Sande and John were about to be transferred from an overseas military assignment back to the United States, their heart's desire was to be closer to John's mother. His father had recently died and, after much prayer, they believed the Lord would station them near her to be of some help.

One day while reading the Bible they sensed a verse leap out as a promise for them: "For the Lord your God is bringing you into a good land—a land with streams and pools of water, with springs flowing in the valleys and hills" (Dt 8:7).

Sande and John longed to go to Ellsworth Air Force Base near Rapid City, South Dakota. "Impossible," they were told.

Ellsworth was under a different command.

When John got his orders to Abilene, Texas, he couldn't believe it. That was flat land, far from his mom. It was not geographically the way the Lord had spoken to their hearts. In their confusion, they chose to hold onto God's Word and trust Him anyhow.

The day before their household goods were to be shipped to Texas, they got a call. John's assignment had been changed. They were indeed going to Ellsworth AFB, South Dakota—a land of hills, valleys, and brooks and close by his mom. Today John's retired but they still live there, on Brookside Street, with a little brook that runs behind their home.

A Decision About Her Children

God cares about families—where they live as well as how they live. He even cares about the education of their children.

After much prayer and research, Elaine and her husband decided to homeschool their three children. They believed God showed them this was their best educational choice for that year. Living in a rural area far from school, they also saw it as a convenience and an opportunity to have more family time together.

But when Elaine's father found out, he was furious. Instead of being happy that his grandchildren would be taught from a Christian curriculum, he screamed ugly names at his daughter. How could she be so narrow-minded? Why couldn't she be more like her older sister, who took her father's advice?

His angry words followed Elaine to bed that night. She knew she had not pleased her father like her sister always did. As she prayed, she heard a soft voice whisper, *"I am the only Father you have to please."*

"What a load was lifted off me," she told me. "My heavenly Father was pleased with me. Maybe someday my father will understand, but even if that never happens, only God's opinion matters. I honor my dad as the Bible requires, but my husband and I listen to God for our family's decisions."

Left Behind to Travel Alone

Sometimes God allows us to be in confusing situations in which we must trust Him for guidance at every turn. Sande's story is a good example.

Sande Lofberg was traveling from her military base three hours north of London with seventy other women to a Christian retreat in Germany. When they arrived at the London airport, all the luggage was taken off their bus—except Sande's purse, with her plane tickets and passport.

Disappointed, she watched the others board the plane for Germany. Once in Frankfort, chartered buses waited to take them to their retreat site another three hours away. Sande was scheduled to teach there the next afternoon. What was she to do? she wondered as she walked through the airport.

"Just trust Me," God's voice reassured her heart. *"Do what you need to do to get the tickets, but trust Me for all your other arrangements."*

The airline agent assured her she could catch a plane at 9:30 that night, but how would she get picked up in Germany and still arrive in time to speak? When the next military shuttle arrived at the airport, she took it back to her base. There she retrieved her lost purse and caught another ride back to the London airport. She boarded the late-night flight and finally arrived in Frankfurt around midnight.

No one met her. And certainly no chartered bus waited to take her to the retreat location. If she took three different trains she could arrive at a town near the retreat center, then call someone to come get her. *"Trust Me, Sande. Just trust Me,"* the Lord had instructed her over and over.

Just as she was about to leave the plane terminal in Frankfurt to head for the train station, a voice barked in broken English over the public address system: "Betty Lasper, meet your party at Gate 6."

"Answer that page," an inner voice said. Sande had to make a quick decision. Yes, she decided, she'd at least check it out.

When she arrived at that gate, a woman was waiting to give her a lift. To Sande she was an angel of mercy and an answer to a prayer. Though the announcer had greatly mispronounced her name—it was nowhere near right—God's urging had made her respond. The woman had arranged a place for her to stay overnight and a ride the next morning with the chaplain and others who were also going to the retreat center.

Sande arrived one hour before she was to speak. Trusting God's voice became even more real to her after that. But she also learned that making decisions about those nudgings was her responsibility.

Coming Back Home With AIDS

"Many Christians are seemingly incapable of listening to God in times of choice, because their spouse, parents, friends, coworkers or fellow church members do not free them to choose well," writes Gordon T. Smith.[3]

Sometimes God asks us to make a decision even amid a lot of outside opposition. We do not feel supported by others.

Instead, we experience their disapproval and judgment. The road to obedience is not always easy. What would you do if you learned that your son, who had AIDS, wanted to move home with his companion, who was also infected?

Dixie faced one of the greatest decisions in her life. Together she and her husband prayed a long time before saying "yes," the two could move into their nearby guest house. Their decision was contrary to the advice of most Christian friends. She wrote me about it:

It has been a dozen years since we became aware of our son's HIV status. At that time not much information was available on the disease. I stayed in disinterested denial—except to God. Mumbling and complaining was my comfort zone. I could vent and there was always agreement from my comforters. Disgust and disappointment became my own sin.

When we first found out about Michael's homosexual lifestyle, I wrote on a napkin at McDonald's: "Lord, I don't know how You can stand this. I thought I could but I just can't." I wrote several paragraphs, signed my name, and sat there, waiting.

The answer was swift: *"Pray! I will show you mighty, inaccessible things that only I can reveal."*

On one occasion, knowing He understood a mother's heart, I asked God: "Do you remember when Michael was a little baby? He was so tiny, precious, and perfect. O Father, I could love him then, why can't I love him like that now?"

Later, another day of frustration arrived. Self-absorbed and critical, I took a long walk and spoke to God again of my concern: "He acts like a little baby boy! Why doesn't he grow up?"

Clearly I heard the still small voice of the Holy Spirit. *"You said you could love him like a little baby. Can you?"*

"I'll try, Lord."

Now I had not just one but two "children." Our son's partner, Rodney, was near my age. He was well educated and aloof.
Aha! I finally had someone to blame. The two of them acted
like husband and wife. I was so offended and complained to
God. *"I have called you to be an intercessor,"* God answered me.

One of my friends counseled me with condemnation. "You
have entertained sin by allowing them to live on your property. Their sin will come upon you." Friends cited examples
from their own lives. I was torn and fearful. I could not offend
God. Yet weren't we to be merciful? Where would they go?
Questions and emotions intermingled.

As my husband and I prayed for guidance, God assured us
that reaching out in mercy to Michael and Rodney was His
plan for us. With this assurance we took the stand of faith in
the midst of friends' doctrinal opinions and harsh judgments.

I could not change these two men; therefore, it was I who
began to change. The Holy Spirit and my husband were always
there, with unconditional love both for me and for Michael
and Rodney.

The disease with its many symptoms and manifestations was
beginning to deteriorate their relationship. Rodney became
more and more depressed, and our son was lost in a haze from
abusing prescription medications. Though our son would not
let me pray or speak about God, he encouraged Rodney to
come to the Bible study class I taught at our house on
Thursdays.

Sitting there—the only man in the circle of ladies—he came
to know and accept Jesus. One prayer was answered! The
women talked to Rod, shared their feelings, read the Bible, and
prayed for him. He had never experienced such a showering of
love. For the first time he was able to perceive women in the

light of the reality of Jesus. He read the Scripture aloud to us, his eloquent diction and resonant voice touching every heart. God's anointing would hover over us. We were all amazed.

One Thursday Rod told me he would not be coming to our Bible study class. "I have to work on the computer at the AIDS task force." Sighing, he took a deep breath and said, "I'm so depressed. Depressed. So lonely."

Our son was now hospitalized for his drug addiction and was not there to comfort him. Rodney's own mind, clouded with the dementia of the disease, was giving in to fear. We didn't see Rod all weekend, and since the cottage was in our backyard, I watched a lot. I left messages on his answering machine. Sunday, as my husband and I left for church, ominous concern churned in my stomach.

The service was wonderful. My thoughts were renewed by the message. As the pastor left the podium, he stopped, quickly turned back, and spoke. His words startled me: "Today some of you will go home and find that the enemy has come to rob you. Don't let him."

I heard the still voice inside of me say, *"He is dead."*

When we got home I called Rodney. No answer. Then I got in bed and pulled the covers over my head, feeling safe. The phone rang. My husband had gone to the cottage and found Rod dead there, obviously at his own hand. He was phoning to tell me.

The next evening I was the speaker at a Christian women's meeting. I spoke of the love of Jesus. My body still trembled and my heart ached, but in the midst of the confusion I felt as though Jesus was there standing with me, unfailing and steadfast. I leaned on His presence in the uncommon remembrance of a man gone home, no longer alone. I felt Rod was truly with Jesus, whom he had acknowledged as Savior. Others around me may have had different beliefs but I sensed Rod was finally home and whole.

"Furious winds often drive the vessel more swiftly into port," wrote British preacher Charles Haddon Spurgeon in the nineteenth century. How furious the winds? I'm still in awe of how victorious we become the more we are buffeted by those winds. And I am still trusting God for Michael's salvation.

At this writing, we have no communication with him. He is in another relationship in another country halfway across the world. Sick and nearer to death from his disease.

Though her own son has not yet become a Christian, this believing mother has no doubt that he will. She has not ceased praying for him.

As for herself, the furious winds of her disappointment have driven her closer into the shore—into the arms of a loving Father who cares for all His children.

Go On Living

My friend Josie hasn't seen four of her grandchildren in a dozen years. When she remarried after the death of her husband, two of her daughters got mad. Not only did they stop speaking to her, they refused to let their children communicate with her either. Even her letters to the grandchildren are returned.

She grieved for a long time over this, but the Lord told her, *"You can't quit living—keep on keeping on with life."* She prays for the day when her family will be restored but in the meantime she is keeping on with life. A hard decision, I know, but she has God's word to her.

Did I Really Hear God?

Probably most of us have experienced disappointments, times when our prayer expectations weren't fulfilled and we grappled with doubt. Did we really hear God?

In our book *A Woman's Guide to Getting Through Tough Times,* my co-author, Ruthanne Garlock, gives a few conclusions she reached when struggling with that question:

Strong desire—even when it's purely motivated—can hinder our ability to hear God clearly. Sometimes when we make a mistake we can simply acknowledge we were wrong about our "word from God," and no harm is done.

But other times, we wrestle to resolve the issue, and the enemy attacks our minds. "What makes you think you heard from God?" he taunts.

Many times over the years I have struggled with this question, and gradually have drawn a few conclusions.

1. In most situations, it's best to have confirmation on my "direction from God" from someone who's not as emotionally involved in the matter as I am. His or her objectivity can protect me from deception. And, of course, anything I feel is a message from God must align with Scripture and with God's character.

2. Even when I do hear God's heart in regard to a particular situation, I must acknowledge that God honors a person's free will. Occasionally a person's wrong choice—mine or another's—can sabotage God's best plan. In this instance, I can ask God to do a work of grace despite the circumstances.

3. In some cases, events later confirm that indeed I had heard from God but was mistaken about the timing. Someone once said, "God is never late—but He passes many oppor-

tunities to be early." It's important to seek clear direction in regard to timing.

4. Sometimes my only recourse is to release to God what I thought was His revealed plan. My prayer becomes: "Lord, I don't understand what is going on. But I release to You my own desires and expectations in this situation. I declare Your Lordship over my life, and I choose to believe that You love me. Please reveal my own attitudes that I need to change, and enable me to do it. Thank you that in the unseen realm, You are working in people and events in a way that ultimately will bring You glory. Lord, my faith is in You, not in my circumstances. Help me to walk in Your peace. Amen."[4]

Not Always Dandy Answers

Sometimes God leads us into a decision where we experience fulfillment and joy as a result of our obedience. Other times He asks us to move forward in decisions that will cost us or cause us to sacrifice some things for a greater good. Sometimes He even asks us to make a decision to move forward, without resolving all the problems we face.

God speaks and when He does it doesn't mean everything is going to be solved in a splendid way. We trust His plan will unfold for our good, and we move ahead believing He is leading us. We will certainly face difficult turning points in our lives. Listen to His voice and trust Him, for He cares so much for us.

Prayer

Lord, I admit that many times when facing a decision, I feel so vulnerable, afraid, uncertain, confused, and sometimes even angry. In my head I know I should listen to You and trust You, yet I find it hard to move forward in my life until I have all the "what-ifs" settled. I can't see the future, but You can. I want to come to a place of trust that with You I can make the right decisions—today, tomorrow, and next year. Please help me grow in my ability to discern Your voice and obey You. I thank You for loving me unconditionally. Amen.

PART 3
When God Says, "Let Go"

૪ચ

I will listen to what God the Lord will say; he promises peace to his people, his saints—but let them not
return to folly. Surely his salvation is near those who
fear him, that his glory may dwell in our land.
PSALM 85:8-9

We must enter into unity with God's will for our
lives through divine revelation. Christ wants our
minds to think His thoughts, our *emotions* to
express His love and our *wills* to choose to allow His
will to be performed in and through us. [This happens as] we cultivate our relationship with Christ....
Fuchsia Pickett[1]

"Trust Me!" God says.

"But it's so hard, Lord," we whisper back.

One of the most profound lessons in our walk with the Lord is learning to trust Him. Do we believe He will handle our impossible situations? Can we place our faith in Him, let go and let Him work?

We long for resolutions. He is the resolution. He is our peace, our Provider, our Problem Solver, and the Healer of broken hearts and shattered dreams. We therefore must learn to abandon our lives to Him—to let go and fully trust Him.

Relinquishing a Child

Sally B. discovered this truth one night—a dramatic middle-of-the-night event when she actually heard the audible voice of God.

I was a young wife and mother and had known God for a long time. But this night, when I woke up suddenly, I didn't know why. My husband was asleep beside me. What could be the matter? I got up to check my baby daughter, my pride and joy. My husband and I had tried for almost five years to have a baby. Now that she was here, she filled my life with such a fullness I had never known. She looked so little, almost fragile to me, and I watched after her carefully.

When I checked on her, she was fine. So I crawled back into bed and just lay there, fully awake now. I stared at the ceiling, what I could see of it in the dark. Suddenly the voice of God spoke to me through the ceiling wall.

Surprisingly, it did not frighten or startle me. I was so concerned with what He said, not that He spoke to me.

"Give her to Me."

I was suddenly filled with sadness. Did it mean she was going to die? If you have never heard these things before, you don't know what *"Give her to Me"* means. So I cried and cried. But I gave her to Him just the same.

I said, "Yes, Sir, here she is," with tears streaming down my face and my face wrinkled with grief. It never occurred to me not to obey the audible voice of God!

She didn't die. She is now thirty-five years old with a wonderful husband and her own two daughters—my favorite and only grandchildren. The Lord has kept her and has been good to her all these years. He is a faithful God.

What was God's purpose in talking to Sally? A simple message: *Trust Me*. While her baby didn't die, Sally's unhealthy fears and clinging did.

When circumstances around us spin out of control, our temptation is to act impulsively, to worry, to try to make the right things happen. God keeps saying, "I have a larger plan and you are not in control." When we hear Him, we have to let go of many things we are comfortable doing, particularly using our wisdom and our timetable. And we must learn to stand in faith that God will work.

The Rescuer Didn't Help This Time

Nancy was always her family's "rescuer." But one day God showed her she couldn't solve every problem they had. Her sixteen-year-old daughter, Rhonda, ran away after a high school football game that weekend. Nancy and Ron searched and prayed for three long days and nights, extremely worried for her safety. Finally she called from a nearby town, asking to come home.

While her parents greeted her with open arms, they realized it would take much love and forgiveness to win a rebellious daughter. That next Sunday in church, Nancy in honest desperation prayed, "Lord, restore my love for her and help me to walk in forgiveness." She didn't hear anything much the preacher said, but God began to pour out His love in her heart for this daughter who had so badly disappointed her.

On Rhonda's first day back at school, the counselor called Nancy. The girl had been so unruly and sassy to her teacher that she had been sent to her office for detention. Nancy was extremely upset about her daughter's behavior. She was praying aloud as she went to the bathroom mirror to comb her hair, determined to go do something.

Looking into the mirror, it was as if the Lord was looking back at her. He seemed to speak: *"Nancy, you don't always have to go and do something. Just let go!"*

"He was right," she told me later. "I prayed but never went down to the school. God knew my nature is to always want to 'do something' or 'fix things.' I decided to let *Him* fix this.

"When Rhonda came home that afternoon I didn't even let on I knew she'd been called into the counselor's office. I just tried to respond to her with God's love, which He had given me for her during the Sunday services."

A mother's prayers and the counselor's words to Rhonda broke through. She straightened up and was much less rebellious the rest of the school year. Years later Rhonda asked her mother's forgiveness for her behavior during those turbulent teen years, when she'd caused such heartache. How many of us are like Nancy, wanting to do something to make the situation turn out differently? But one look in the mirror and hearing

God's voice can change a plan of action immediately. That is, if we are listening, as Nancy was.

Give God Your Expectations and "What-Ifs"

As God's children, we have to let go of our wants, fears, expectations, anger, hurts, disappointments, even our "what-ifs." We must totally abandon our situation into the Lord's hands.

A beautiful young woman I know had a difficult decision, not unlike many women her age growing up in this generation. She finally came to a place where she knew she had to let go of a relationship with no assurance it would be restored.

Letta had lived for three years with Mitch without commitment or the blessing of her church or family. Since she was raised in the church, she knew marriage is God's highest goal for a couple who love each other. One day, knowing the Lord was displeased with her lifestyle, she heard Him say, *"Will you love Me and trust Me? You have saddened My heart by your choice."*

"The Lord would talk to my lonely heart," she remembered, "asking me when I was going to be His. I went through a deep depression and could not make Mitch understand why I was sad.

"Finally, I took the leap of faith and moved out. My friends warned I might lose Mitch. But I decided I loved God more. I knew by this time what I needed. After I moved I had real peace and no fear. I'd made the right choice."

She decided that even if she never saw Mitch again—a man she truly loved and admired for many of his fine qualities— she'd rather be pleasing to God. But Mitch loved her and they began dating. He started going to church with her and, before long, he too gave his heart to God. Five months after Letta moved out, they were married. Today they are active in church, committed to God and to each other.

"I am sure there will be other times I will have to trust God with my situations—and the outcome may not always be as sweet, but God will always be with me!" she told me.

Letting Go of Broken Hopes and Dreams

Can there be healing after a broken dream? A broken heart? Yes, according to Audrey, who walked through it.

Audrey was a junior at a Bible college when she renewed an acquaintance with Ben, a friend she'd met the previous summer. He was doing graduate studies and they were both pursuing music ministries.

Ben was handsome, talented, and godly. As their relationship blossomed, they spent more and more time together. He played the piano for her while she sang, and they performed together both on campus and at local churches on the weekends. Sharing their dreams and hopes, they often talked of marriage. They even got to know each other's parents rather well. Their relationship seemed "God ordained" ... or so Audrey thought.

But they differed over some doctrinal issues, and this conflict tore at Audrey's heart. Why does this have to be an issue? she wondered many times. She grieved over it, and it was about to split up her perfect dream.

"It was too painful for me to see God's full picture," she told me. "Finally, the Lord showed me our doctrinal differences were not the root of the problem. I was. I was not waiting for God's dream for me, for His perfect plan."

Audrey knew she had to give up Ben. God was requiring her to trust Him for His better way. Was obeying God easy? Not for Audrey, not at first. Her senior year was the most painful of her life. She couldn't mention Ben's name without crying. "Oh, God, I obeyed Your voice. Fill the emptiness in my life— the hole left from Ben's absence," she prayed over and over.

God's promise to her from the Word was all she had to stand on: "I know the plans I have for you ... plans to prosper you and not to harm you, plans to give you hope and a future" (Jer 29:11). She read it over and over.

Audrey graduated and moved as far from campus as she could get, and found a perfect teaching job in an area she loved, beside the ocean. Though she often wondered about Ben, she came to a place of contentment with the Lord.

"Then, in my contentment, I met Marshall one day in church. It seemed the Lord was just waiting for me to totally abandon myself to Him, regardless of the cost, before He would show me His next step," she said.

"Marshall, as it turned out, was more than my 'wish list' for a husband. My list was dinky compared to God's quality one. I didn't know that I needed someone to keep me laughing, to remind me to enjoy life when I get too bogged down with work, to truly cherish me and fill my heart with incredible joy. We even sing and minister together. I find that the more I let go—of my ideas—the more the Lord does awesome things for me," she said. Audrey and Marshall have been married for six years and are now involved in an overseas ministry.

Audrey had to make a decision based on God's word to her. She let go of her dreams and hopes and waited for God's better ones.

A Mom Who Heard God's Whisper

Many of us get outside advice on how to handle a crisis. But in the end, it is God we must count on. Maryanne shares her story of a daughter in a troubling medical situation.

My daughter Susan, who had graduated from college, was now home living with us while she worked. I knew she had battled bulimia for ten years. Now I noticed how extremely thin she had become.

Though she sat at the table with us and ate an abundance of food, she would later go to the bathroom and deliberately throw it up. She was obsessed with the fear of being fat. My husband and I and our five other children became alarmed about her condition. Panic gripped me when my close friend, an experienced nurse, told me bluntly, "Your Susan is going to die if you don't do something now. You'd better hospitalize her immediately."

I didn't want to be blind to what was happening. Nor did I want to move outside God's will for my daughter. Because she was twenty-three, I knew if she wasn't willing to go to a treatment center herself, I would have to take legal steps, declaring her incompetent in court and becoming her guardian, then having her admitted to a facility against her will. This would definitely damage my relationship with her and perhaps affect her future employment opportunities.

Of course I was more concerned with her state of health. I wanted her to live, not die. Thinking my nurse friend might be right, I began making phone calls to locate a Christian treatment center. I finally found one that was two thousand miles away that might soon have an opening.

I talked to Susan about possible hospitalization. "Please, Mom, I will do anything, just don't put me in a place like that." I could not get peace about sending her to a treatment center, especially to one so far from home. I was unsettled in my heart about this choice.

So one day, after much prayer, I determined to stop looking at her thin body and to shut out all voices except God's. That meant voices of my friends, my family, even my own. I began to seek the Lord for His particular plan concerning my daughter's health.

That morning, after she left for work, I climbed up into her bed, embraced her pillows and prayed earnestly for several hours. I asked God's protection over her and His plan for her health.

"No hospital," God whispered to my heart. I "listened" with my spirit and a deep peace began to settle over me. God was assuring me He wanted to heal her without hospitalization.

During the next two days, He began to reveal His plan. I was to start Susan on a system of nutritional supplements. He even showed us the name of a Christian doctor nearby, who agreed to accept her as a patient. Then she began to talk to me honestly about her past at school—when the kids called her names, how isolated she had become—after she had shared with them in the seventh grade how God had healed her miraculously of asthma.

She had never told us about her shunning. She had sat alone at school in the classroom, cafeteria, and library for years. The trauma of isolation was one root cause of her bulimia, we discovered.

Today Susan has gained some weight and looks so much better. She is carefully following her nutritional support plan. I believe we are at least halfway through our tough times. The more she opens up to share with me, the more she is healed and, I think, less likely to fall back to her old patterns.

I am grateful that I listened to God's voice and His plan. I am believing Him for her complete restoration.

Letting Go of Deep Emotions

Sometimes one of the hardest areas to "let go" is that of our heartrending emotions. We want to hold tight to our "right" to disappointments, anger, unforgiveness, and more.

This next story tells about the remarkable journey of a second wife and how she let go of feelings concerning her husband's first wife—no easy matter, but God helped her achieve it.

Rosie and Johnnie had both been married before. He had five children from his first marriage; Rosie had one. Since a great deal of their income went to pay child support for his children, who lived with their mother, resentment built in Rosie to a boiling point. She tells her story:

My husband's first wife, Monique, took us to court every few years to get more child-care money. She tried to turn her children against me, though I did everything to show them love. Then my husband and I became Christians and I started praying in earnest for Monique and their children.

When their oldest daughter wanted to get married, I took in extra work cleaning houses and saved for a year to pay for her wedding. But at the wedding it was Monique who had the prominent place as the mother of the bride, enjoying the fruits of my labor. I was hardly acknowledged.

Johnnie and I got legal custody of one son when he was twelve. He eventually joined the Army and met a girl he loved. While making plans to get married, they learned she was pregnant. When Monique got wind of it, she suggested an abortion. But Johnnie's son was horrified by the idea. He himself was adopted and had been born just before the legalization of abortion. He knew he could have been aborted by his unwed biological mother. He wouldn't consider that option. They were married in our living room by a pastor from our church. Monique came looking like a bomb about to blow up.

A few months later my husband and I attended a revival meeting. While there, the Lord convicted me I needed to forgive Monique. I was holding her and myself in bondage. I was giving Satan a foothold in my life. I felt like a rag doll, leaning against the altar rail in the auditorium that afternoon. I wanted to forgive Monique—because I wanted to please God. But it was so hard!

Then I heard Him say to me, *"Are you ready to let it go? Will you give it all to Me?"*

"Lord, I choose to forgive her," I whispered. I left the meeting excited about my decision. But when I got home I found myself still talking about the things she had done to me. Suddenly I realized that every time I spoke about her past offenses I opened all the wounds again. Where was forgiveness?

"God help me," I cried.

The Lord impressed on me the need to write Monique a letter, asking her forgiveness for holding onto my resentments against her. The letter arrived at her house just a few days before two of our grandchildren were to be in a Christmas play. I didn't plan it that way; it just worked out.

When I saw her at the church service, I walked up to her and threw my arms around her. To this day, I can't tell you why I did it, unless it was God's leading to show her I had truly forgiven her. After that, her cutting comments about me became fewer and fewer as we attended the same family gatherings. Finally, I could truly say I had come to love her.

Recently she called to invite me to a Christian women's conference. Though I couldn't go, I thanked her and promised next time I would. When I gave it all to God—just as He asked me to in that revival service—He took it. Miraculously, I bear no more animosity toward her.

Bill's Timing Out of Order

What do you do when God speaks to you specifically in answer to a long-breathed prayer? Obviously, there is a right time to share it: too soon could abort it; too late could make you miss the opportunity. Bill discovered—almost too late—that it is possible to lose his word from God. He shares:

During my college years, I didn't date. I was busy with my studies and didn't have much money. I told God I wouldn't date anyone until He showed me the one He had for me to marry. I wasn't interested in dating because it seemed so shallow, and when I dated I wanted it to lead to marriage. After three years at the University of Wisconsin, I began to be discouraged, wondering if He would answer my prayer.

After my junior year, I left for Oak Ridge, Tennessee, for a summer training program. One Saturday morning some of the trainees working with me asked me to go with them to a Catholic church picnic at a nearby lake. There I met her!

Lou arrived with one of her friends, who had insisted that she come along. I was wearing my Wisconsin pin with the phrase "We Like It Here." When Lou saw it, she told me, "My roommate is from Wisconsin."

As Bill heard her voice speak to him, he heard another voice he believed was God's say, *"This is the one you will marry."*

Their friendship continued to grow, since Lou was staying home for the summer, working as an aide in the local hospital. They spent many hours walking all about Oak Ridge. One day, just six weeks after they'd met, Bill handed Lou a letter.

"Here, read this," he said. As she read, he poured out his heart, telling her she was to be his wife.

"It scared the socks off me," she told me, laughing. "I thought Bill was rushing things too quickly. I was only twenty and I wanted to finish nursing school."

Right there on the sidewalk, their relationship almost ended. Lou had been hurt in several relationships in the past and was not at all interested in any commitment. They decided to keep their friendship going by letter and phone calls as each returned to college.

A real test of Bill's faith came when doctors examined Lou for possible cancer. If he had heard God correctly and she was to be his wife, surely she couldn't die, he reasoned.

"Thank God the tests were negative. During this time, I was forced to trust the Lord that His revelation to me was true. At times things looked very bleak, but eventually our relationship blossomed," Bill told me.

Lou earned her nursing degree from the University of Kentucky. Then Bill was drafted out of graduate school and headed for Vietnam. But at the last minute his orders changed and he was assigned duty in Virginia instead. They then decided to get married, two and a half years after Bill had heard the audible voice of God telling him Lou was to be his wife.

After almost twenty-nine years of marriage—and five children—Bill says, "The Lord has blessed us abundantly."

Letting Go of Grandchildren

There is a saying that goes, "When you've done all—stand." That's where our next woman found herself in letting go of a situation with which some grandparents may identify. She shares her heartbreaking dilemma.

We raised our children to know and love the Lord. I never thought we would have to deal with a teenage pregnancy. But at age fifteen my daughter Miriam was pregnant. She talked about placing the baby for adoption. I told her that I would support her decision, but if she brought her baby home I would be too attached to part with him or her later.

She did bring her home—a tiny, sweet, five-pound girl. I was hopelessly in love with Suzanne from the moment I saw her. Miriam quit school during the pregnancy. Now she was nursing the child and still could not go back, so they continued to live with us.

Then one day my daughter just left home, leaving her baby behind. I got Suzanne on a routine. She was so good and so easy to love. She went everywhere with me; we were constant companions. It was such fun to watch her learn about everything—birds, grass, flowers, dogs. For two years she brought a long-needed joy into my life. We laughed, sang, and played together.

Then Miriam had a second child—a plump, happy boy— and she was back living at home. Again I helped care for him and fell in love with him. Now two-year-old Suzanne slept in the room with my husband and me due to lack of space in our house.

Miriam married the father of the second child. She and the children still lived with us. Her husband visited during the day and once in a while slept overnight. When my grandson was four months old, they decided to move out of state and be a family. I had mixed feelings. I wanted them to get their life together, but it was torture to part with the children. I prayed that the Lord would keep them safe. The day they left, I cried all day.

We called regularly when they got to their new home. But it got harder to find them at home so we could talk. Then one day I learned Miriam had placed the children for adoption as soon as they had arrived at their new home. When I heard that, I ran into the bathroom and threw up. Tears streamed down my face. I felt as if part of me had been torn away. My heart ached. My body ached. How could she give up the babies I loved so dearly? Why didn't she just leave them with us? They were ours. They were mine.

My husband flew into action. He called a lawyer. For days we explored, asking several agencies probing questions, contacting a child-find group. And spending lots of money. Finally we concluded that legally we didn't have a chance to get them back. We wanted to keep fighting, though. One day as I poured out my heart to God, begging Him to return the children to me, He made it clear that I had not asked Him what He wanted.

I prayed, "Lord, make my will Your will."

A great peace fell over me when He said, *"Let them go...."* I didn't understand it all, but I yielded.

My anger toward my daughter began to fade into sorrow for her. I then realized she had given up not only her children but also her family—her mom, dad, sister, and brothers.

For days after I'd found out my precious grandchildren were gone, I'd grieved as though they were dead. Now, with a word from God, a hope began to grow. Somehow I knew they were in His care.

God impressed me to call our daughter and tell her I loved her no matter what. Compassion had replaced hatred. She asked forgiveness and I gave it. It lifted a huge burden off my heart, and I am sure off hers as well. She let them go so they'd have a better life than she could give them, she assured me. She would have always felt guilty if we had had to raise her children—and resented us for putting them ahead of her, she said.

The Lord opened my eyes to see her pain, her sorrow. She was my child and she needed to be first in my life, over them. She also wanted them to have parents who could give them everything—emotionally, physically, spiritually.

Today I know they are in a godly home with several generations of godly ancestors. My grandchildren are the answer to prayer for a married couple who trusted the Lord for ten years to receive one child. He gave them two.

We send pictures, letters, and gifts to our grandchildren through their adoptive parents. And we receive pictures and letters from them in return. I still sometimes cry when I walk through a store and see children's clothes and toys. I still cry on their birthdays and at Christmas because I miss them so. I long to hear their sweet voices. But I know God is in control. I have learned to live in a place of trust in my heavenly Father that I never knew before. I'm quicker to fall on my face and ask my Father what to do now. I now know His ability to turn sorrow into gladness and to give me joy for mourning.

Many people told me that they would never have given up trying to get them back. I would have said that too if I didn't know how wonderful it is to walk in the peace that comes from yielding to the all-wise God. In addition, the Lord is restoring my relationship with my daughter in a loving way. I see her through His eyes more each day.

When we feel so "out of control," how much easier it is to turn the wheel over to God and let Him steer us where He knows it is best for us to go. Letting go isn't always easy, but as we've learned from those who've shared here, it is the only way to discover how wise, loving, and capable is our God with all that concerns us.

Prayer

Lord, how I truly want to let go. To trust You more fully. To surrender to You all my impossible situations. But I admit that, more often, I hold on too tightly. Please help me to learn to trust You so completely that I can know without a doubt that You have a better answer to my problem than I can imagine. Thank you, dear Lord and Savior, for caring about every aspect of my life. I pray in Jesus' holy name. Amen.

PART 4

God Speaks to Us About Money

ଙ୍କ

[Jesus said,] "Do not store up for yourselves treasures on earth, where moth and rust destroy, and where thieves break in and steal. But store up for yourselves treasures in heaven.... For where your treasure is, there your heart will be also."

MATTHEW 6:19-20a, 21

Money never made a man happy yet, nor will it. There is nothing in its nature to produce happiness. The more a man has, the more he wants. That was a true proverb of the wise man, rely upon it: "Better is little with the fear of the Lord, than great treasure, and trouble therewith."

Benjamin Franklin[1]

God really does care about every aspect of our lives, even our pocketbook.

He is not opposed to our having money. But He is opposed to our being greedy or allowing money to become an idol in our lives. The Bible says the love of money is the root of all evil (see 1 Timothy 6:10). Our Father wants us to have our hearts and wallets aligned to His purposes and He then blesses us! One of God's names is Jehovah Jirah, God our Provider. Many Christians consider that everything they have belongs to Him. They are just stewards, or caretakers, of it.

But sometimes, when God is not operating on our timetable, we may think He's forgotten us. Maybe you know people like these who seemed actually robbed by circumstances. Here are a few I know:

- A grandfather falsely accused has to give a lawyer $30,000 to defend him. The elderly man drives a rusted-out truck because what he'd saved for his new car went to a lawyer for something he didn't do.

- A couple struggling with infertility must come up with $20,000 to adopt a baby and put off buying their first home.

- A young man, home from the mission field after ten years of service, finds it hard to "start over" in supporting his growing family. The job market underwent change while he was gone. No one seems to want to hire him, despite his college degree and talents. The bills pile up.

- A woman with three children is left with hardly enough money to meet their bills when her husband moves out so that he can marry his secretary.

But God wants us—whether we feel like a victim or victor—to know His comfort, His direction, His voice, and, yes, even

His provision. All of these people mentioned eventually saw their money problems worked out. While the money wasn't all restored, God sustained them. Amazingly they all rested in trust that God would provide.

Mounting Medical Bills

My daughter Quinett's roommate and prayer partner, Cathy, was a single working woman facing impossible financial problems. She'd had emergency gallbladder surgery and her insurance company would not cover the medical bills.

One night, as they prayed together about the enormous debt, Cathy told Quinett, "I believe the Holy Spirit has shown me we need to do spiritual warfare over this." They knew how to do that. Quinett later told me about it.

"We came against the powers of darkness, demanding them to loose money for Cathy's medical bill," Quinett said. "We had no idea where the money was coming from, but we continued our warfare for about thirty minutes. Finally we felt total peace about it, so we went to the kitchen and cooked supper—sure that somehow Cathy's bills would be paid."

As the weeks passed, the bills kept coming from the doctors and the hospital. Cathy skipped meals so she could send small, regular payments. Then began the phone calls saying her accounts would be turned over to a collection agency if she didn't pay up soon. But she maintained the God-given peace she'd felt when she and Quinett had prayed months earlier.

One day Cathy got a letter from her insurance company stating they definitely would not cover any of the costs. Cathy turned to a coworker and said, "It doesn't look like my insurance will come through, but God will."

The colleague rolled her eyes as if to say, "Yeah, Cathy. Like how?"

Eight months later, without any explanation, the insurance company sent a check to cover 80 percent of the costs. By this time Cathy had paid the rest. What caused an insurance company to reverse its decision?

Cathy and Quinett can only say they did what the Holy Spirit led them to do, and God took care of the rest.[2]

A Daring Trust to Tithe

Sometimes God asks us to do something rather daring regarding our finances. Corrine tells her story of bold obedience, then of the blessings:

I was a new believer and, while my husband was stationed in Europe, I attended the U.S. military chapel. During one of the services, the chaplain read, "Will a man rob God? Yet you are robbing Me! But you say, 'How have we robbed Thee?' ... 'In tithes and offerings.... Bring the whole tithe into the storehouse, so that there may be food in My house, and test Me now in this ...' says the Lord of hosts, '... if I will not open for you the windows of heaven, and pour out for you a blessing until it overflows. Then I will rebuke the devourer for you....'" (Mal 3:8, 10-11a, NAS).

The chaplain explained that, if we bring our tithes to God, He will pour out a blessing on us and rebuke the devourer for our sakes. I was already giving a tenth of what I earned at my job. But my husband was not a believer, so we didn't tithe on his income. God convicted me in that message that, regardless of my husband's unbelief, we were to tithe on both our salaries.

I clearly heard Him. I had no choice but to ask my husband. Frankly, I was afraid to face him, then to consider what it would mean to us financially. After all, he was in a low-level rank and my income was not that great either. What would he say to me? Would he be furious?

When I finally got up enough courage to ask him, his response was, "Tithe on the whole thing?"

"Yes. Everything that we get from our jobs, from gifts, from our folks."

I could see fear come upon him, then anger. But after a while that subsided. He finally agreed, "OK, but if the car breaks down, or we need new tires, or if anything goes wrong, I'm taking that money and we're going to pay our debts."

I did not respond to this because I wasn't in agreement with his statement. I knew what the Lord had told me to do and I was going to do just that. Within a short period of time, everything my husband had mentioned that could go wrong, went wrong. The car needed new tires, we had to replace the car's transmission, and we incurred various other unexpected bills. In spite of this, I continued to tithe our income, since I was the one who wrote the checks for the bills. I don't know how God managed to stretch our money, but He did. We were able to cover all our debts and to pay our tithes.

A year later, when we had moved back to the States, we had another major car expense. This one totally drained our finances. I was not working at this time. We had just gotten my husband's paycheck, but the debt from our car and from normal living expenses such as telephone and insurance left us with only a few dollars in the bank.

When I realized that we had no money and still needed to buy food for the next two weeks, I started to panic. But I'd been reading in Exodus how God supplied the needs of the

Israelites as they left Egypt. God immediately reminded me of what I'd been studying. He had supplied their food and water. Even their shoes did not wear out. Every need they had was taken care of by God Himself.

I knew that He was challenging me to believe and trust in His Word. Since He is not a respecter of persons, I said to the Lord, "OK, just like You took care of the children of Israel, I believe You will do it also for my family. I will not try to do something on my own. I will just trust in You. You will have to increase what little I have in my cupboard."

Within an hour the doorbell rang. When I went to answer it, no one was there. But there was an envelope stuck inside my screen door. On the front of the envelope there was a note that said, "Praise The Lord." When I opened it up, I found a $50 bill inside. I had no clue who God had used to deliver it. I told my husband, "See, God has done this for us. He will not let us go without." I waved the bill as I spun around in joy.

"Oh," he replied. It was all he could think of to say. But I knew God had registered this gift in my husband's heart and, sometime in the future, He would reveal to my husband the record book of His faithfulness to us.

For the next twenty years I was faithful to tithe. I thought I had really achieved a great measure of faith in God. Then one day panic gripped me again. This time I read that the U.S. Social Security system might be bankrupt by the time I reached age sixty-two. We had spent our lives in the military, living from paycheck to paycheck. We had no savings and we didn't own a home. Now I began to worry, big time! I couldn't sleep. I had night sweats and I was constantly in fear, doubt, and unbelief. No Social Security for me, when I'd need it?

Then God spoke to my heart and reminded me that He had never failed me. Every time we had had a financial crisis, somehow we had made it through. We hadn't missed paying our bills. We hadn't gone hungry. I was so sorry that I had momentarily forgotten His blessings to our family. I asked Him to forgive me for my doubt. I told Him that I would trust Him for our future financial needs.

Two weeks later I was in my church. It is my custom to place my tithes and offerings in the church envelope. After it is sealed, I kiss the back of the envelope because giving is an act of worship and I purpose in my heart to worship God fully in this way. As I placed my offering in the plate, like a flash the Lord spoke to my heart, *"This is your Social Security plan."* He then showed me a vision of myself twenty years earlier, making a decision to tithe on our entire income.

All these years I had been obedient to His Word. I had given our tithes into God's Social Security plan. He had taken that money—which was His anyway—and added His interest. I had unlimited resources in the bank of heaven, so He would make certain that I would lack nothing. Whatever I was counting on for Social Security, God would meet it.

In the Malachi Scripture on tithing, the Lord said to test him and see that He would open the windows of heaven and pour out a blessing. Now that I have been married thirty years, I continue to see God's faithfulness. My mother recently died and left me a small inheritance, which we used as a down payment on our first house ever. Our daughter, who nearly died as a teenager, is now grown. She, who was diagnosed as infertile, has seen the Lord grant her the desire of her heart—two precious children.

You may not think this has anything to do with my decision to tithe but I think it does. God's blessings overflow in our lives, just as He promised.

Needing Help out of a Financial Mess

Finding herself in a financial boondoggle she'd created, Lane cried out to God to rescue her. In the process, God helped change her heart and attitude toward government and taxes.

I told myself I was seeking God's direction about my finances. But what I did was ask God to let me buy a Laundromat as a tax break. It was a selfish wish, since I was looking for a way not to pay so many taxes as a working single woman. After all, most of my friends had businesses and did not have to pay taxes.

After a year I hadn't done well financially. I decided to sublease it, but found I couldn't get my name taken off the lease. The owner of the property was adamant: "No way." I still owed $7,000 on the lease and had a business that wasn't paying off. I went to my lawyer and tried to get him to do something. God began to change my heart and my attitude. I prayed a lot and I repented for being angry about having to pay the IRS. It looked like I was stuck with a losing business.

One day in prayer I said, "Lord, I've already signed a three-year lease. I admit I've really messed up. I don't think this was Your plan for me. If there is anything You can do, please get me out of this lease. If You do, from now on I won't begrudge the government any of my taxes."

Finally, my lawyer sent some legal papers to the man who owned the building, again asking if I could sublease it without my name remaining on the contract. It was a last-ditch effort since all my phone calls to the building's owner had produced no results.

When the Laundromat owner read the legal jargon in the paperwork my lawyer sent, he called me up. I could tell he was willing to negotiate. "I'm not hiring an attorney to interpret what your lawyer has written out. Our contract is void and you are out of it. Lady, don't contact me again—ever," he barked.

When I got that call, I shouted and thanked God. Then I asked the Lord to be my financial advisor.

Even in our mistakes, when we repent and are honest with God about our desire to get our finances under His control, I believe He honors our effort. At least He heard my prayers in that instance. No one else might see it as a cause for celebration, but I did.

The Trip Looked Financially Impossible

I usually recognize the sweet, quiet way the Holy Spirit speaks to me. But sometimes He just won't let me let go of a "prayer burden." I hang onto it like a dog with a bone. During these times all I can do is pray, asking Him to bring a solution.

While attending a conference in another state, a burden wouldn't leave me. For several days I'd spoken often to three women—close friends from different states—who were there as intercessors for the conference. I kept telling them I was concerned because our friend Barbara, who was there with us, was leaving for Asia in less than three weeks to speak six times. And she was going alone.

Another friend, Judy, who was also at the conference, was willing to go with her and had indeed been her prayer partner on other overseas ministry trips. Judy's husband was willing for her to go. But every time we discussed the possibility, Judy's response was, "I'd go if there was money to go, but we don't have it."

"Just believe with me for it," I'd tell her and the other

women with us. "Jesus sent His disciples out two by two and I have a strong impression Barbara needs a prayer partner on this trip." Not only was there no money for Judy to go, time was short to get a ticket on the same plane.

"It really helps to have a friend along to pray for you while you speak and to have someone with you when you change planes and trains in a foreign land," Barbara admitted.

Just before I was to catch my plane home, Barbara and I ate lunch with a mutual friend, a businessman who'd been attending the conference. Soon we were both relating exciting stories about Barbara's many adventures around the world, some of which I'd shared with her.

"She's leaving soon on another overseas trip, speaking six times, but she is going alone," I told him. "Her prayer partner, Judy, is willing to go, if there were only funds for her plane fare."

"How much would it cost?" he asked Barbara.

"I really don't know. I got my ticket several weeks ago."

"Here," he said, pulling a business card from his wallet and handing it to Barbara. Contact this person at our office. I'd like our organization to invest in your missions trip."

Barbara was flabbergasted. I was thrilled. We had just a few moments to rejoice over how God had worked this out. God had put the concern on my heart and caused me to share it with those few prayer team members. Then I'd mentioned it during our lunch conversation with the businessman, surprising even myself when I did so. I had no clue God would use him to be the answer to Barbara's need for a traveling companion and prayer partner.

Two and a half weeks later, Judy and Barbara were flying over the Pacific. Their combined ministry had a powerful effect on fellow believers whom they encouraged during the many meetings held in a nation where only a small percentage of the population is Christian. They also reached nonbelievers.

Money was really not a problem. We simply needed the Lord to guide us to His source.

Single Mom Gives All

Jan remembers a time when she was a single mom and extremely low on money.

While attending a revival meeting one night, I kept feeling deep within my spirit that God was telling me to give all that was in my checking account.

I argued, "But God, you know I only have $7.15. If I give all of it, how will Matthew and I eat?"

I could not shake the feeling that God Himself was asking me to do this. By the end of the evening, I wrote the check and deposited it in the offering basket at the back of the church as we left. I didn't even tell Matthew what I'd done. But God knew; He saw my willingness to obey His prompting, even though it left my bank account empty.

When we got home, I found four sacks full of groceries sitting on my back porch. We'd been showered with such a variety of food—far more than I could have ever bought with $7.15. Things like steak and shrimp and fresh vegetables. I never learned who brought it, but it taught me to trust when I hear God's still, small voice and to obey. He can be trusted!

A Lesson in Radical Faith

Many years ago Ray joined a ministry that was having worldwide impact. At a conference for leaders, a speaker named George described what it meant to have radical faith in God.

After the meeting, Ray challenged George.

He told him he felt the message was overstated and some of his hypothetical situations of "radical faith" seemed foolish, perhaps even dangerous. George simply met Ray's objections with passages of Scripture on how to respond in faith to all kinds of difficult circumstances. Ray left, shaking his head but continuing to wrestle with what he'd heard.

Two weeks later Ray found himself seated across from George at a dinner meeting. After the meal, George pulled Ray aside and said, "A few days ago, I went to the bank to cash the check I had received as an honorarium for speaking at the conference you attended. As I was in line for the teller, the Lord spoke to me to keep the cash in an envelope because God had a purpose for it.

"Tonight," he continued, "as I sat down across the table from you, I knew immediately that the Lord wanted me to give you the envelope. Please take it." He pushed the envelope toward Ray.

"I can't take that money. You and your family need it," Ray said, feeling terribly awkward.

"The Lord takes care of us. This is His plan for this money," George replied.

When Ray continued to refuse, George put the envelope on the table. As he walked away he said, "You can fight this out with God, Ray."

With tears in his eyes, Ray realized how badly he needed to have the kind of radical faith in God's provision and care that George had. He reached down and took the envelope. When he got home he put the envelope in his dresser drawer without opening it. The gift seemed like something sacred, and he did not know how to deal with it.

A few weeks later Ray's wife was in the hospital after

delivering their second daughter. When he went to pick up his wife and baby and pay the medical bill, he found it was significantly more than he had expected. He did not have enough money to cover it. Then he remembered the envelope in the dresser. He went home and opened it. To his amazement, it contained the exact amount he needed to pay the hospital bill. God's message came across to him loud and clear.

The barriers of unbelief in his heart had been broken. He was launched on a journey of faith that made his ministry and leadership over the following years incredibly fruitful. George heard the Lord speak. Because he obeyed, God was able to impart to Ray the faith he so longed for and needed.

How to Finance Five College Educations

For Mary Elizabeth, getting a word from God meant giving up her own ideas of how her children would get an education, then standing firm in her trust in the promises God placed in her heart for her family.

Over the years I've found that if I have a word from the Lord—whether from the Bible itself or one that He speaks to my heart—I can make it through just about anything.

My husband and I have five children, including a set of twins. Because I was concerned about their future college educations, I fully planned to return to nursing to help with those hefty tuition bills. I'd been a nurse for four years before my first child was born, but every time I determined to go back to work, I'd find I was pregnant again. I decided to wait until the first child was almost ready for college, then I'd return to work.

One day I was again seeking the Lord about their educations

and my nursing skills. He spoke very clearly to me that I was to do two things: give Him my desire for a nursing career; and stay at home to mother my children and keep them covered in prayer. I felt He showed me that each child had a special calling.

"You teach them and pray for each one to enter fully into the plan I have for that one. If you do this I will fully provide for them to go to college," He impressed on my heart.

I can't say that I accepted this word joyfully; it was a big disappointment to give up nursing. But after grieving and pouting for a few days, I agreed to obey His word to me. Within a few months my longing for a nursing career was gone. Now I wanted nothing more than to stay at home, pray for my children, and teach them everything I could about God's Word.

During my oldest daughter's senior year in high school, we began investigating colleges and asking the Lord which one He wanted her to attend. Though the finances looked impossible, she chose a small Christian college that would help her prepare for her dream of being an overseas missionary. She had some scholarships, but there remained a balance of $4,300 to be paid in a few short weeks.

I knew the Lord had promised *full provision,* and He is always faithful to His Word, but storms of doubt and guilt seemed to rage all around me. We barely had money for groceries, much less her college tuition. My daughter was becoming increasingly frustrated and upset about it—wondering if I had *really heard from the Lord at all.* I would retreat to my room to seek the Lord, read again the Word He had given me years before, and try to regain strength for the battle. But I knew God had spoken to me.

About ten days before the trip to take her to college, my husband was in an accident. The long trip was too much for our damaged car, and the insurance settlement was too low to buy another car. The picture looked dark indeed. But faithful friends stood by me in prayer as I kept trusting in God's word to me.

A few days later we learned our daughter had won a $4,300 grant for her first year of college. The exact amount that we lacked was being sent directly to the college. Then we learned the insurance company of the man who had hit our car had decided to cover the rental on a minivan so we could transport our daughter to college. Every need was met.

Since then we've had three children in college at the same time, and God has faithfully provided for each one. I know God will provide for my last child when her time for college comes too.[3]

Mary Elizabeth's oldest daughter has since graduated and married. She and her husband have just left to serve as "hidden" missionaries in a country where Christians are persecuted, even tortured and killed.

Count on God's Financial Direction

Truly, if we listened like Mary Elizabeth and stood on God's Word, we could count on Him to give direction for every financial decision we face. But it isn't just finances He wants to speak to us about. I like what David Wilkerson wrote about listening:

> The early Christians did not walk in confusion. They were led by the Holy Spirit in every decision, every move, every action! The Spirit talked to them, and directed them in their every waking hour. No decision was made without consulting Him. The church's motto throughout the New Testament was: "He who has ears to hear, let him hear what the Spirit has to say."[4]

I have a friend who says she trusts the Lord Jesus with her financial decisions—and she always consults Him before her stockbroker—because He is a great bookkeeper, far smarter at figures than she is.

God truly wants us to experience an abundant life here. But He also wants us to lay up treasures in heaven, where rust does not corrupt. When we give to Him, through tithes and offerings, or to others in His name, we are obedient children, pleasing to our Father God.

Prayer

Lord, when I acknowledge that all I have is Yours—including my money and material belongings—then I must become a better steward of what You have entrusted to me. Sometimes I want to hold on to what I think is rightfully mine. Forgive me for such foolish thinking. I thank You for every blessing You have poured out upon me. Thank You, dear Lord, for You are the Giver of every good and perfect gift. Amen.

PART 5
When God Tells Us to Pray

⧼⧽

If any of you lacks wisdom, he should ask God, who gives generously to all without finding fault, and it will be given to him. But when he asks, he must believe and not doubt....

JAMES 1:5-6a

Talking to men for God is a great thing, but talking to God for men is greater still.

E.M. Bounds[1]

Often God burdens us to pray for others when we don't have full knowledge about their situation. Perhaps we may not have even one clue, or we may have just a bit of the puzzle.

You've had the experience before, I'm sure. Someone's name comes to mind, or you have a vision, or you get a deep down inner impression. You stop to pray for that person. Though you don't know the reason you were alerted to pray, you did, right then. These are times of trusting and praying, even if we feel we are praying "in the dark."

You may say, "Holy Spirit, I'm not sure how to pray. But would You show me?" Or, "Lord, I come boldly to Your throne of grace to intercede for my friend. Please intervene. Show Yourself strong on her behalf. Whatever her need right now, I stand in the gap and ask You to please meet it. In Jesus' precious name I pray."

Battling in Prayer for a Son's Deliverance

Carmen is a visual person, so God usually shows her pictures in her mind and she's then faithful to pray. One hot evening fifty people crowded into their south Texas home for a prayer meeting. As it neared the close, her thirteen-year-old son Emanuel called his dad to come get him from a friend's home.

When they got home, Emanuel threw his backpack in his bedroom and joined the others in the living room. As soon as he walked in, Carmen knew something was wrong. "God, what is it?" she prayed.

"Emanuel brought something into the house that is not holy," God seemed to tell her. She went to his bedroom and, as God directed her, rifled through his backpack. Then she pulled out a pornographic video and took it to her bedroom. After the

guests left, Carmen showed her husband what she had found. They agreed to pray about it before confronting their teenager.

The next day they faced their son with the evidence. They told him they knew he was using the small television set in his bedroom not just to play Nintendo but to watch blatant pornography.

"But I need my privacy," he responded angrily.

"Privacy is a privilege. When you abuse it, you lose it. Your father and I have established the standard of Christ in our home. You live here by that grace," his mother told him.

After learning the video belonged to a friend, Emanuel's father returned it to the boy's parents.

Emanuel's behavior continued to show his parents his mind needed renewing. As Carmen prayed in his room, she anointed the television set there and in essence commanded that no more unrighteousness be released through it. Three days later it literally blew up, with a big puff of smoke!

His parents began a concerted prayer effort for Emanuel because they knew pornography was just one reason for his rebellion. Carmen enlisted other prayer partners who came to their house to pray for the boy without being critical of him as a person. She says this was a key—no judgmental attitudes— just caring for a son who needed the Savior. Sometimes they'd sit on his bed and just sing praises to God.

Realizing they were in a spiritual battle for their son, they wrote Scripture verses on paper and placed some around his room, even between his mattresses and on top of the fan blades, fighting with the Word of God. This was a passage Carmen clung to: "Can plunder be taken from warriors, or captives rescued from the fierce? But this is what the Lord says: 'Yes, captives will be taken from warriors, and plunder retrieved from the fierce; I will contend with those who contend with you, and your children I will save'" (Is 49:24-25).

Meanwhile, his parents showered Emanuel with love but kept ever mindful of his need for parental watchcare. Whenever there was a hint that something was amiss, Carmen would get a "picture" from God and confront her son. She was always accurate.

Their prayer effort was not easy. Sometimes discouragement set in. But two years later Emanuel asked his parents for their forgiveness. He regretted getting into pornography and asked prayer help for his deliverance and healing. They prayed over his mind and thoughts and he was set free.

Father Warns Son Beforehand

Author and counselor John Sandford has helped many learn to hear from God. One day he sensed danger for his son Loren. When he asked God about it, he was given a vision of Loren swinging down from a high place, using long yellow lines. Of course, he stopped and prayed for him.

At the time Loren was doing some carpentry for a friend who was building a house on a cliff above the Spokane River, with a boat dock and garage below. Before the young man left for work, John told him about his vision and urged him to be careful.

That day, Cynthia, wife of the man building the home, and two of their daughters came out to inspect their new house.

Cynthia squatted by the edge of the cliff to examine something about the foundation. A powerful, invisible hand hit her in the back with such force it tumbled her over the edge of the cliff! She hit on her heel and then lit on her back halfway down the cliff on a ledge. The girls took a long yellow extension cord and lowered it down to Loren, who had clambered up that steep, shale-covered cliff side to reach Cynthia. Loren was a weight lifter at the time. Having tied the electric cord about his waist, he took Cynthia in his arms, trying desperately not to move or jostle her spine, for fear it was broken, and stepped down that steep incline, balancing precariously with Cynthia in his arms. With the girls steadying him by pulling on the cord, he made it safely all the way down, and put Cynthia in the back of the station wagon. At the hospital it was determined that Cynthia had fractured three vertebrae, but not one had slipped out of place! Any one of the three could have sliced her spinal cord. Her right heel was sheared off. But the heel and back were so soon healed that within three weeks she was swinging happily along on crutches without a cast.[2]

This true-life adventure was just as John had seen it in his vision, and he had prayed for the safety of all concerned.

When to Give a Word to Someone Else

Sometimes when God shows you something about someone else, it isn't always "good news." Often He reveals hidden things to Bertha when He calls her to pray for someone.

Bertha doesn't necessarily share the information with the one involved, unless she has prayed about it for a while. If she then believes that God is saying the appropriate time has come to warn someone of trouble, she will.

Once she felt God showing her that a spirit of lust was overtaking her friend Nora's husband. When she shared this with Nora, her friend admitted she had suspected this for some time. She was struggling to work overtime to pay the bills that kept coming in.

Now Bertha and Nora prayed together for truth to be revealed. Finally Nora's husband admitted he'd been supporting another woman—and was committing adultery.

The story didn't necessarily have a happy ending, but Nora was thankful she was alerted before she contracted a sexually transmitted disease. The courts ordered her husband to contribute to her financial support.

If the Lord is giving you a warning, it may just be for you to "war" over during prayer. Several times when I've received impressions about trouble or difficulty concerning someone, I have continued my prayer effort without sharing the information.

This was especially true when our three children were all teenagers and many other youngsters were in and out of our home. The Holy Spirit would show me how to pray when I knew no actual facts.

She Prays for an Acquaintance

Sandra often wakes in the middle of the night to pray. One particular night the Holy Spirit led her to pray for Toria, a woman she knew only as an acquaintance. Sandra didn't know where Toria was or what she was doing at the moment, but she felt an urgency to contact her. She sent an e-mail message.

"The Lord has me praying *to protect His plan* about whatever you are doing now, so I am interceding."

Later she learned that during those crucial hours, Toria was meeting with Christian leaders in another nation, seeking a prayer strategy for their country. As a result, some critical decisions were made on how to reach that nation for the Lord.

"Though I was thousands of miles away, I was included in their plan," Sandra told me, relating how much Toria had later thanked her.

Cries Out for Son Far Away

Jody tells about her prayer efforts on behalf of a son when she had no natural knowledge anything was wrong.

One Thursday morning I became troubled about my oldest son, Lewis, who lived far away from us. I kept trying to reach him by phone and at work. I left messages, but he did not return them. By the weekend I knew in my spirit that the situation was critical. I continued to phone. Finally, one of his coworkers told me he was home, not feeling well.

I found myself on Saturday afternoon alone in the house; our other children and my husband were out doing errands. I stepped into my kitchen to get a cup of tea.

Like a flash of lightning, a holy boldness came over me and I began to declare: "Alcoholism and drugs—you are not taking any member of my family, especially Lewis. You are not going to kill them. I stop you by the authority of Jesus Christ." The odd thing is I had no knowledge that any of my sons were into drugs or drinking. However, Lewis had tried both in past years.

On Monday Lewis called from a hospital room in Seattle. He told me that the week before he had learned his girlfriend had aborted his baby, which he had wanted very much. He was so devastated that he left work on Friday, bought some liquor, and went home to drink. By Saturday night he was so out of it he didn't care what happened to him. One of his roommates came home and suggested that they do drugs. He said OK. By then, he said, he didn't care if he lived or died.

By Monday he said he should have been dead—due to the amount of drugs and alcohol he had consumed. He'd tried to overdose. But two friends became concerned about him. When they got to his apartment and found him passed out, they immediately took him to a hospital.

He called me when he was on his way to recovery. Thank you, Lord, for hearing a desperate mother's cries.

God Warns of Her Children's Danger

Iloa, mother of three, had a similar prayer alert when all her children were out on a river. She wrote me:

My son, David, was taking the youth from our church in Wisconsin on a tubing trip on the Apple River. This was his first trip as the youth pastor. Robin, his fiancée, was visiting from California, and was excited to be going along. My teenage daughters, Susan and Kathy, were also on the trip. The late summer weather was absolutely gorgeous, a perfect day for tubing down the river.

My husband, Ralph, and I were working out in our yard, raking and cleaning up around the trees. Suddenly the Lord spoke to me, "Your children are in great danger." I looked at my watch. It was almost two o'clock. I called to Ralph, "We've got to stop and pray. Something is going on with the children. God showed me that they are in danger."

We paused and prayed for protection for all on the youth trip. Even after we returned to our yard work, I kept praying until they finally arrived home in early evening.

"What happened at two o'clock?" I immediately questioned David.

"Oh, a freak storm hit about then. It might have been a tornado."

His sisters filled me in on the details. The storm had struck suddenly as they were tubing down the river. The wind was wild. Lightning was flashing. Trees were falling in every direction. A blinding rain fell in icy sheets. With no place to go for shelter, everyone crouched down by the rocks along the shore. Several of the young people and chaperones narrowly escaped the falling trees. God had miraculously protected all of them from serious injury and death.

I'm glad God speaks to us, even when we are busy at work.

Pray for the Gates of Your City

I'm glad too that He alerts us to pray about situations we don't understand—at least not at the time. Marsha, who lives in a city surrounded by several military bases, tells of an experience when she was called to pray for her community:

One morning I heard the Lord say, "Pray for the gates of your city." To be honest, I wasn't sure what the gates of my city were. But I began to pray for protection. I prayed against terrorism. Against natural disasters. I prayed for safety for those who lived here. I cried out for God's mercy. Then I prayed that God would seal the gates of my city. I continued to lift up this need all during the day as I went about my business. Truly I didn't understand, but I obeyed.

That night on television, I heard an announcer say that the

army base within our city limits had received an anonymous threat. All gates were shut and the highest level of security was ordered. No disaster occurred. No bomb was found. No terrorist attacked.

Who knows how many others may have also been alerted to pray that day?

Gulf War Alert

Another woman told me how she was alerted to pray one night for a specific country during the Persian Gulf War. She explains:

Suddenly I became quite agitated. My heart beat fast and my palms were sweaty. This was unusual because I'm a very calm person.

I asked God what was happening. I heard Him say, "Israel is in danger. You must pray. Now."

So I went into my bedroom, got down on my knees by the bed, and began to pray for Israel. I prayed. I wept. I pleaded. My whole being seemed engulfed with the prayers for the safety of Israel.

After a while, I felt peace. I went back to the living room. A little later, the television program I was watching was interrupted by a newscast saying that Tel Aviv had been bombed by Iraq. Only one man died—of a heart attack. Not one single person was directly injured or killed by the fierce bombs.

Praying when we have no full knowledge is really moving in obedience to God. We are listening, even when we don't understand the reasons.

Mysterious Plane Change

Have you ever been in a dangerous situation and come very close to death? Perhaps you learned afterward that not only did God protect you, but other people were praying for you without knowing any details of your situation.

Leonard Crimp was a sixty-five-year-old salesman who was about to retire. He had just spent three weeks training his successor, traveling with him to various parts of Canada. They ended up on November 29 at Saint John, New Brunswick.

After lunch that day, they were looking forward to taking an afternoon flight back to Montreal, then home to Windsor. They learned their afternoon flight had been canceled because of bad weather. They could take a bus to a town some ninety miles away and catch a later flight from there. But the bus was leaving in just a few minutes.

Hurrying into his hotel room, Leonard was glad he'd already packed. He shoved his New Testament in the middle of the suitcase and closed it shut. He and Jack rushed to get onto the bus. Away they went.

When they got to Fredericton, a plane was waiting and they got on board. They realized that, because of the delay, they were not going to reach Montreal in time to make connections with their flight to Toronto and then to Windsor.

Once in Montreal, those who were making a connecting flight to Toronto were told to follow an airline representative to gate forty-one. Just before they arrived, the rep asked, "Is there a Mr. Crimp in this group?"

"Yes," he answered.

"Oh, I am so very sorry. I should have told you before—but there is a seat on flight 724 which leaves from gate 7." What a blow. He had already walked from nearby gate 5 where they first arrived. He knew by the plane number it wasn't a jet.

"I've been traveling with my sales companion here. We want to get home together," he told her.

"You'll be in Toronto about the same time. You won't have any delay," she assured him. "But your luggage will be on this plane."

Leonard was not one to argue, so he said, "All right."

"Jack, I'll see you in Toronto," he called as he began his walk back to catch the smaller plane. When he finally arrived at that gate, passengers had already boarded. Almost out of breath, he approached the attendant at the desk.

"Where did you come from?" the startled man asked.

"From flight 403 from the Maritimes. I was going to flight 831 but they sent me back here."

"How confused can they get?" he said to Leonard, scratching his head and checking his passenger list. He picked up the phone and made a call. Finally someone told him to go ahead and put Leonard on board. As soon as he was seated, the doors were closed and the plane took off.

Leonard arrived in Toronto safely after a somewhat turbulent ride. While waiting in the airport to catch up with his friend—and his luggage—on the other plane, he learned the sad news: flight 831, the one he was to have been on with Jack, had crashed four minutes after takeoff. Everyone on board had been killed, all 118.

Imagine how surprised he was some days later when authorities returned his New Testament—mangled a bit—from the plane wreckage. Nothing else from his luggage was found.

He was so glad to be alive. Only later he learned about intercessors who had prayed for him.

His sister-in-law in Winnipeg had called his wife and said, "I know Leonard is traveling and the Lord has put him on my heart and I've been praying for him." A widow from his church had driven twenty-five miles in her old Volkswagen to tell his wife, "It is strange but I was up all night praying for your husband." Three others wrote that they were praying—two he barely knew. The staff at the Gideon office met and prayed for him four days before the fatal crash.

"The only thing you can say after having something like this happen is, 'Lord, you've got something for me to do, what is it? Lord, lead me, guide me, and keep me,'" Leonard said.

A few months later, after he'd trained another successor, he retired. But he didn't stay retired. He soon embarked on a second career, working with the Gideons, an organization known for distributing Bibles. He traveled to fifty-two countries—all by airplane—and served for a long time as president of the Gideons in Canada.

Leonard Crimp died at age ninety-four, twenty-nine years after he planned to retire as a salesman. He often wondered if the confusion the airline clerk had complained about was really God's divine plan to save his life.[3]

Lots of Answered Prayers

Aren't we glad that others hear God for us too? Most of us will never know until we get to heaven how many prayers were offered up to God by those He alerted to pray for us. Perhaps we'll even get a clearer understanding of some surprising events that happened on earth because we were faithful to pray for others when we didn't really understand at all.

We continue to learn to be alert—to stop and pray—even when we do not have full knowledge of the whys involved. Becoming obedient to His call is what's important, especially if it seems we are praying without many facts.

Prayer

Lord, You said when we lack wisdom, we are to ask You. Please give us wisdom to know how to pray as we ought. May we believe and not doubt Your voice when You speak to us. Let Your Holy Spirit pray through us even when we don't understand the whys and hows involved in the lives of those we pray for. Lord, help us be obedient and to trust! We ask in Jesus' name. Amen.

PART 6

His Assurance in Difficult Times

℘

For we do not have a high priest who is unable to sympathize with our weaknesses, but we have one who has been tempted in every way, just as we are—yet was without sin. Let us then approach the throne of grace with confidence, so that we may receive mercy and find grace to help us in our time of need.

HEBREWS 4:15-16

The last and greatest lesson that the soul has to learn is the fact that God, and God alone, is enough for all its needs. This is the lesson that all His dealings with us are meant to teach; and this is the crowning discovery of our whole Christian life. God is enough.

Hannah Whitall Smith[1]

All of us will experience difficult times that test our faith. Some difficulties will scare us. Many of us will lean into God as our reservoir of strength. Still others may become bitter and turn from God.

God is intimately aware of our trouble and struggle. He's the Shepherd going through the valley of the shadow of death with us.

I heard a pastor say, "The pressure of difficulty will bring out what is in us—either to turn us toward God or away from Him, into hopelessness and discouragement. We can grow more during tough times if we will allow Him to walk us through them." Even in our difficult times, He's there waiting to speak, if we but listen.

To Live or Die

My friend Cindy Edwards recalls a time when she had to hear God's voice clearly for her daughter.

When my daughter Stacey was sixteen, she became gravely ill. She was initially admitted into the hospital because she had a high fever and was vomiting. The military doctors where we were stationed in Berlin could not diagnose her.

At first, the doctors thought she had a virus or flu, but with each passing hour, her condition worsened. Life was ebbing from my beautiful teenage daughter. Several doctors called their alma maters in the States, describing her condition in hopes that some medical expert might be familiar with the symptoms. No one seemed to be able to shed any light on what was wrong.

Knowing the situation was grave, I slipped into the hospital chapel to be alone and to pray. "Lord, tell me, is my daughter going to live or die?" His answer would make a difference in how I prayed.

"If she is going to live, Lord, I will stand on Your Word, no matter what I see. But if she is going to die, I need to know because I am going to be very mad at You and I want to deal with that anger now—ahead of time—so I will be able to call on You as my friend and Comforter when she dies."

I knew I would be holding the Lord at arm's length at a time I did not need to be asking Him to forgive me of my anger. But I didn't get an immediate answer to my question. News of Stacey's illness had spread through the entire military base. Christian friends and strangers kept coming to the hospital to encourage me with Scriptures on healing. "That's nice," I'd think, as one after another read the Bible to me. No specific verse penetrated into my spirit.

Within three days, the doctors decided to medivac her to a large Army hospital in another part of Germany, as her condition was now critical. They said that she was dying but they were unable to determine the cause. I was still questioning God, but I had no answer.

My chaplain dropped in to see me the night before we were due to fly out of Berlin. "God gave me a word for you three days ago, but I was afraid to give it to you," he said. That was exactly the day I had prayed and heard no answer from God. "You will find it in John, chapter eleven, especially verse four."

I opened my Bible to the passage as he'd instructed, and I found myself reading the story about Lazarus' death and resurrection. The fourth verse said, "This sickness is not unto death but for the glory of God."

As soon as I read this verse, I felt like someone had poured a bucket of joy into me. I knew that the Lord was telling me that Stacey would not die. I looked at her limp form in the bed and thanked God for this messenger who had come to me with such great hope.

After my chaplain left, I looked at my watch and thought, "Oh, I need to get to the Post Exchange before it closes and buy her a beautiful nightgown because she is going to live."

As I was stood in line to check out, the clerk asked me how she was doing.

"She's great!" I responded.

"Is she better, then?" the clerk asked.

"Oh, no. Not yet. She looks terrible, but God said she's going to live," I assured her.

A doctor standing behind me who had been on Stacey's case looked at me as though I was crazy—certainly a delusional mother who was hoping for the best. I went back to the hospital and within four hours after I had experienced such joy and hope, she became delirious. She'd talk like a normal sixteen-year-old and before her sentence was finished, she'd be babbling baby talk. I became terrified.

Was it possible that just four hours earlier I had believed the report of the Lord and yet now, with one circumstance, I was terrified of losing my daughter? The Lord spoke to my heart once again. He said, *"You asked for something to hold on to and hold on is what you are going to have to do."*

I knew He was saying that this illness was going to be long and drawn out. That brought comfort to my heart and I was able to sleep. We were flown to a better-equipped medical facility in Germany. Even after we arrived, her condition continued to worsen. In the cardiac intensive care unit she was hooked up to numerous machines; IVs flowed into her veins, delivering fluids and four antibiotics at one time. Chest tubes were inserted in both lungs and an NG tube went from her nose to her stomach.

For twenty-six days she lay in bed in critical condition. All that time her doctors told me she was dying and I should prepare for that outcome. They had no answers as to what was causing her illness. The antibiotics were killing the bacteria, but the illness was releasing toxins that were going through her vital organs. She developed pancreatitis and hepatitis. By the time the illness had finished its course, she had lost two-thirds of her lung capacity.

Slowly she began to improve and was able to endure painful physical and respiratory therapy. One night it took her twenty minutes to walk just six feet. But she cried and praised God that He helped her do it.

After forty days in the hospital, she was finally released. I often recalled God's Word to me that she would not die and that He would be glorified. I lost count of the number of Christians who said that their faith had been strengthened by Stacey's healing. Hospital doctors as well as the others on the military base who were not Christians also saw the power of God in action.

God Speaks in Her Crisis

Mary describes how God chose to speak to her through a Scripture verse during her crisis.

For months I'd helped a young mother of three as she battled cancer. I saw firsthand the ravages of this horrible disease.

On the day of her funeral, my doctor called me with personal bad news. I'd had a recent mammogram; now he was recommending I come in for a biopsy on a small, suspicious breast lump. Doctors wanted to remove it surgically. Because I wanted a second opinion, I went to another doctor for an examination. He agreed with the first doctor. "Wait no more than two weeks for surgery," I was told.

My family and friends surrounded me with prayer—in person, on the phone, and in small prayer groups even when I wasn't present. The day I was to go in for the biopsy, I was led to read Luke 1:30 in my Amplified Bible. The Lord spoke tenderly to me as I read: "And the angel said to her, Do not be afraid, Mary, for you have found grace (free, spontaneous, absolute favor and loving-kindness) with God."

Of course I knew that was what the angel said to the Virgin Mary. But on August 23, 1990, the Lord said it to me, through His Word. My heart was filled with joy and peace.

My husband drove me to the hospital and I was fully prepared for the biopsy. More X rays and sonograms were required, so I went through them. I asked my doctor if any woman had ever not needed her biopsy. It might have happened, he said, but he just didn't know.

I was being examined again when the nurse asked me, "Now which breast is it?"

After more discussion and examinations, I received the good news: "You don't need a biopsy." The lump, the doctor explained, seemed to have become translucent and had shrunk.

As we went to tell my husband, I told the doctor about the many people praying for me. He listened politely. "I like telling good news," he replied, smiling, as he reached out his hand to shake my husband's.

When we told my husband, he and I broke out in tears simultaneously. But they were tears of joy. Indeed, that day my comfort was "Fear not, Mary."

Hold On to God's Word, Regardless!

Shortly after Bet became a Christian in the early 1970s the Lord began to speak to her as she read through the Bible. She shares her journey.

I'd sit down and read His Word as a starving man eats a great meal. One powerful passage the Lord spoke to me had a profound effect on our whole family: "They shall not labor in vain, Or bear *children* for calamity; For they are the offspring of those blessed by the Lord, And their descendants with them" (Is 65:23, NASB).

This verse sprang to life for me on April 18, 1973. Our three sons were teenagers. Several months after receiving this promise from God, we discovered our oldest son, age sixteen, was a drug addict.

For the next few years we walked with him through drug rehabilitation programs. At low points of discouragement I would read this Scripture—my Scripture—and cry out to the Lord: "Oh, Lord, this is such a calamity. You said that I did not bear children for calamity."

One day as I was praying about it again, the Holy Spirit whispered to me, *"This is not a calamity. Not knowing Jesus Christ is a calamity."* From then on I had faith to believe for the salvation of all three of our sons and for our descendants yet to be born.

The years passed. Our son Pete was in full recovery, engaged to be married to a wonderful young woman. At the Lord's nudging, I bought them a beautiful leather-bound Bible as an extra wedding gift. Inside I marked the text Isaiah 65:23. Neither he nor his fiancée were Christians at the time.

Five years later they were expecting our first grandchild, our descendant. But his wife was having trouble in delivery. The doctor wanted to do a cesarean section because the baby's birth position was feet first.

Pete came out into the hall and asked his dad to pray that God would turn the baby. Several of us stood in a circle and prayed, asking God to be merciful. Even as we prayed, the baby turned in her mother's womb.

Moments later a nurse rushed out and called Pete to come into the birthing room if he didn't want to miss his baby's birth. Our granddaughter was born beautiful and healthy. Later Pete told me after Susan's birth he began to read the Bible I had given him for a wedding present. He said he was excited to see that in the margin by Isaiah 65:23 I had written, "Claimed April 18, 1973." Susan was born on April 18— sixteen years later to the day I had claimed my descendants for the Lord.

God has been faithful to His Word. All our sons have come to the Lord and several of our grandchildren too. Listen, God wants to tell you something too.

God's Assurance on Her Saddest Day

Connie writes about the worst day of her life:

The saddest day of my life was on a Friday in 1996, when my husband and youngest son came to tell me that my precious, firstborn son had taken his life.

This handsome, intelligent, gregarious, Christian attorney—husband to a wife he adored and the father of two little preschool boys—ended his life six weeks prior to his fortieth birthday. He had shown no signs of depression. Just that morning he and his dad had breakfast together and there was no indication this was the last time they'd be together.

All of the whys, what-ifs, and if-onlys would come later. In that moment of agony, which only parents who have lost a child can understand, the Lord spoke to my heart as clearly as if it were audible, *"This one is home. He is with Me!"* Through the trauma of activity necessary to the closure of a funeral, those words resonated from deep within my being. My Father carried me through this nightmare as surely as if I had been physically lifted, wrapped, and nestled through the long, tedious ordeal.

The wrappings were the prayers, love, and concern of God's people who locked their shields of faith around us, in order that we could even survive.

In my anguish, I cried out for answers. Again came that still, steady voice of my Father, *"You dedicated him to Me at his christening; and you relinquished him to Me in his teens. He is Mine."*

I certainly don't understand. I grieve. I miss that precious son of mine. But I live and move in what God spoke to me, *"This one is home. He is with Me."*

The Enemy Tries to Steal Her Joy

Another mother faced a difficult time following her son's untimely death. She told me about it:

Our oldest son, Terry, age eighteen, had died just two weeks earlier during an asthma attack. He'd had asthma since he was two, but the shock of losing our teenager was so surprising and unexpected. It was hard for me as his mother to accept.

As a family, we'd decided not to go to the Christian retreat at Strawberry Lake in northern Minnesota this year as we usually did. It was just such a grieving time for us. But Christian friends convinced us that our family needed to get away and that the week at camp would be a good time for recuperation and relaxation. So we went.

The first night at camp, our sixteen-year-old son, Craig, returned from the evening youth service with a burning fever and severe pain in his neck and back. After losing Terry, I was panic-stricken at this sudden illness.

Family and friends from the camp prayed for Craig. Finally we all went to bed. During the night, I woke suddenly. I felt that he was in grave danger. I went to his bed to check on him. He was still burning with fever and moaning in his sleep.

Satan spoke to me, "I took your first son, and I am claiming your other four children."

Fear took over. I returned to my bed just a few feet from Craig's cot. I continued praying for several hours. I begged God to save Craig and our other three sleeping nearby.

Then God spoke to my heart, *He shall live and not die.* Eventually, I drifted into a peaceful sleep. After all, the Lord Himself had comforted me. When I woke at seven o'clock, I looked across the room for Craig. But he was not on his cot. I found him at the kitchen table eating breakfast. His fever and pain had left.

At the end of the week after we'd returned home, I called our doctor and shared the symptoms that he had experienced. To him it sounded like either meningitis or encephalitis. He was amazed that our son had completely recovered so quickly!

A Ride Turns Into Near Calamity

Marilyn was driving when her husband, Arthur, had a traumatic experience.

They were returning to Virginia from a Christian Ophthalmology Society prayer meeting in South Carolina. When they pulled over for gas, they decided they'd take the more scenic route instead of the freeway and Marilyn offered to drive. They'd also agreed to snack instead of stopping for a hot meal.

Arthur was eating bananas and lots of raw almonds. They chatted. Marilyn wondered when they'd arrive home. Arthur said maybe in less than a hour. Then, while he talked, he seemed to fall asleep. When Marilyn poked him she realized he was unconscious.

She pulled into the driveway of the nearest house and yelled at the man outside, "Call 911! My husband needs an ambulance!" It seemed like forever before the rescue squad arrived. Arthur was making snoring sounds. He had turned blue and his tongue, face, neck, and arms had swollen. Beads of perspiration were on his forehead. Marilyn put some cool paper towels on his head and mopped his brow.

"I immediately started praying and calling on the name of Jesus," she says.

Jerry, the man who had called the ambulance, kept taking Arthur's pulse. When Marilyn was sure he was dead, Jerry said, "His pulse is still strong." From all outward appearances this was hard to believe. But it was the hope she needed to hear. The ambulance team gave Arthur the oxygen so vital to keeping him alive.

Jerry drove with Marilyn to the hospital some twenty miles away. On the way, she became a prayer warrior in a deeper dimension than she had ever experienced.

She gives the details:

First I was asking Jesus' help in a very modular tone of voice. Then it was as if the Lord placed a huge whip in my hand and said, *"Use it."* I bound the spirit of death over Arthur and I loosed the spirit of life over him in the name of Jesus.

I even heard myself bellowing loudly, "Satan, you will not have my husband because I stand in the gap, in Jesus' name."

God dropped a Scripture in my remembrance, "Not by might, nor by power, but by My Spirit, says the Lord."

I prayed for wholeness in my husband's body—that he would not even be disabled. Then aloud I made a confession of faith, "Lord, you are Alpha and Omega—the beginning and the end. You have our days numbered; only you know the beginning and the end for each of us. Lord, I love my husband and I ask you not to take him from me."

As soon as Jerry and I were ushered into a "family room" to wait, I called our son James to pray. He in turn notified several prayer chains. Soon after these people began interceding for Arthur, he regained consciousness.

After many tests doctors concluded he had not had a stroke or a heart attack. That left two possible conclusions: he had an allergic reaction to raw almonds or he choked on the handfuls of almonds he was eating. Arthur and I both praise God for sparing his life, and for a stranger willing to help us.

Learning to Trust God Through Cancer

Joslyn operates a small beauty salon in her home. The first time she hit rough times, she had no one to turn to but herself. Eight years later, when her second crisis threw her a blow, she sought God's mercy with great faith, simply because she'd turned to God.

I was a Mary Magdalene of the l970s—a loose woman. For eleven years I searched for love in all the wrong places, hopping from bar to bar and cowboy to cowboy, living a promiscuous lifestyle. Looking for love from a man, I never really found it.

I became a "women's libber" after I realized I was not ever going to get married. One day after I had turned thirty I went to the Planned Parenthood office to get a pregnancy test. When they told me I was pregnant, I was probably the only one there who was really delighted. In my fantasy world, I thought I'd be happy now that I would have someone—a child—to love me.

Since I had come to believe that I didn't need a man on a permanent basis, getting married to my baby's father never entered my mind. We were not sweethearts. But to have a baby was going to be a wonderful experience. Little did I know what lay ahead.

After my son was born, my mother came to help me for the first two weeks, but my parents lived three hours away. As a single parent I didn't get the luxury of sleep, which is critical, especially as a hairdresser with no sick leave. Finding baby-sitters was difficult.

But with all that goes with tending to a baby—bottles, cloth diapers, tantrums—I was soon brought to a physical and mental halt. When my son was seventeen months old, I returned to my church roots. Deep inside I knew I needed for-giveness. I also knew my son needed a spiritual anchor. I began a search. God found me and gave me the rest and worth I had been looking for. Like Mary Magdalene I was saved, forgiven, and cleansed—by His love.

I grew spiritually, both at church and through Bible study

groups. Relying on God as my Husband, I started talking to Him aloud—asking for His help.

Then, when my son was eight, I discovered a lump on my breast. The biopsy showed it was cancer. After I got home and took pain pills, I walked over to my bed and studied the picture of Jesus hanging on the wall. I am always drawn to the thorns on His head and the look of compassion in His eyes. Tears welled up in my eyes. *"I loved you enough to go the cross. I took your suffering,"* the Jesus of the painting says to me.

One night as I lay on my bed looking again at the picture, I prayed. "Lord, hold my hand." I lifted it up. Amazingly, I felt a squeeze. Overwhelmed with worry, I wrote out my prayer requests and prayed constantly. Who would run my shop? Who would take care of my son? Would the doctors get all my cancer? How long would it take to recover? Finally I had to embrace trust—trust in my God. I finally located help to run my business and a baby-sitter, and I scheduled surgery.

Both breasts were removed. Following the surgery, pain was my companion. Nights were hardest—the crushing pain felt like an elephant standing on my chest. Soon after the mastectomy, I underwent a hysterectomy, then chemotherapy.

This road was the toughest. It was like being in a bus going down a mountain without brakes or steering. There was the constant vomiting and other difficult physical side effects from the drugs. I learned during this awful time that Christ really loves me and I can trust Him.

Nothing is wasted in God's economy because what I had experienced as a single working mom, God used to plant a desire in my heart to help others. Now I often have the opportunity to share in church groups, on the radio, and in Christian magazines in order to encourage single moms that God can make something beautiful out of their messes.

Singing Again Just to Please God

When her mother was nearing death, God told Marie she had entered the School of Trust. "I began to search the Scriptures for verses on trust," she wrote me. "I wrote them out on index cards, meditated on them, memorized them, and even wrote songs for some of them. This way I could sing in the rough times—of which there were many."

Marie went through other heartaches and family illnesses. The final blow came when her daughter, a beautiful young mother, died of cancerous brain tumors. During each trial Marie had made the choice to trust God through yet another tough time. But this was different.

She had believed God for her daughter's complete healing. When it didn't come, she felt totally cut off from God and spiritually numb. She even questioned whether God was real or not.

"I had no idea how hard my faith would be hit—for I was one who had never doubted the promises of God," she said.

God asked her—as an act of trust—to begin to sing again. To Him, for Him, and finally for others in the churches where she'd once sung beautiful solos.

Marie began, at first just as an act of love for her Father. She sensed no life or heart to her singing. Gradually, with God's help, she's experiencing victory. She sings because her melodious voice is God's gift to her. And it's one way to please Him.

I share her story because many of us go through tough times and, when God asks us to do something that was once "second nature" to us, it seems impossibly difficult to do, even in obedience to Him.

One may lay down a brush and say, "I'll never paint again."

Or, "I'll never write again." Or a wife betrayed and abandoned may think she can never love again.

In Unsure Times, God Is Our Only Hope

John Hagee says it well: "When times are unsure, there is only one sure hope—God. Not rank or position. Not military might. Not reputation. Not wealth. Not political friends. Not social status. All these power plays are empty when it comes to building a sure foundation for life, especially eternal life.... But the Lord is able and sure to help."[2]

Drawing strength from God makes our way through trauma possible. He wants to be our refuge, our fortress, and our Comforter.

Prayer

Lord, I admit I don't do well in difficult times. They test my faith and most often I fail. Yet during those tough times, I lean more and more into You. Too often I forget that You are just waiting, longing to speak to me. But I'm too absorbed with my difficulties and can't hear You. Help me to be more open, obedient, willing to hear even in my pain. Thank You for Jesus' pain and His willingness to die in His difficult situation so that I may live eternally with You. Amen.

PART 7

God Prepares Us for Life's Losses

୫ଚ

[The Lord] has sent me to bind up the broken-hearted ... to comfort all who mourn ... to bestow on them a crown of beauty instead of ashes, the oil of gladness instead of mourning, and a garment of praise instead of a spirit of despair....

ISAIAH 61:1b, 2b, 3b

We need a renewed awareness of death, yes. But we need far more. We need a faith, in the midst of our groaning, that death is not the last word, but the next to last. What is mortal will be swallowed up by life. One day all whispers of death will fall silent.

Philip Yancey[1]

One of the most profound crisis points in life is when we lose a loved one.

To see one we love leave us permanently is an earthshaking experience. To embrace a hope that there is a God who cares for us, who speaks His comfort, who gives us glimpses of eternal life—even in the midst of our loss—is faith.

God and God alone can take our grief and make something beautiful out of it. How? you may wonder. Wait until you walk through such an experience and you will discover it yourself. I did.

Something to Cherish

Have you ever felt you'd reached the end of your endurance when a stranger came along to offer some cheery advice that cut you to the quick? If so, you'll know how I felt, standing outside the nurse's office on a Friday afternoon that spring.

"I'm sure your mom will say or do something so special you'll always cherish the moment. In fact, you'll be glad you took her home from the hospital regardless of the hardship it may be to care for her and watch her suffer," the social services nurse told me pointedly.

"But I don't understand," I protested, leaning against the door. "I've been taking care of Mom for a year now while she's fought a losing battle with this cancer. I just can't take any more. Besides, I don't have anyone to help at home."

She pushed a slip of paper into my hand and said warmly, "Here's a list of nurse's aides who work in homes. Try calling Harriet first. I think she's available. She's certainly experienced. I'll arrange for a registered nurse from the health agency to check your mom at home a couple of times a week."

Trying to sort my thoughts, I stepped on the elevator and mashed the button for the fourth floor, where my seventy-two-year-old mother was a patient.

When I'd brought her there by ambulance two weeks before, the doctors were sure she was just hours from death. Yet she dreaded dying in a hospital.

"No heroics. No life-saving equipment. Just keep me comfortable," Mom had told her doctor as he examined her bloated body right after her admittance. But the doctor, bound by medical ethics, ordered everything he felt she needed to make her comfortable—antibiotics, oxygen, heart medicine, diuretics, intravenous solutions.

For the past twelve months Mother had been fighting cancer in the lymph nodes. The doctors never found the primary source. When it was first discovered, this strong woman, who had single-handedly raised four children, did what she'd done all her life. She committed her situation to the Lord. Dozens of friends stood with her in prayer.

Later, when the pain became unbearable, her oncologist suggested, "Let's try treatment now."

"My hope is not in chemotherapy—it is in the Lord. Whether I live or I die, I'm the Lord's," she told him, finally agreeing.

She submitted to chemotherapy and radiation, with all their horrible side effects. Twelve different times I checked her into the hospital fifty miles away for three to five days of chemotherapy. I slept beside her there every night. I saw her through six weeks of radiation treatments as an out-patient there, driving her back and forth daily. My husband and I also moved into her home to care for her around-the-clock.

Mom and I both knew she was nearing the end of her fight. She was too weak this time to ride the fifty miles to the hospital where her oncologist and nurses who knew and loved her could help. Her new doctor in our local hospital said he could no longer keep her in the hospital. They needed her bed. Her condition was stabilized.

My sister Ann, who'd been there for two weeks to help keep a twenty-four-hour vigil in the hospital room, was returning to her family. I was to take Mom home. Again. Home to die, I knew.

"Lord, give me strength to bear it. Don't let me let her down. Help me," I prayed as the elevator slammed to a halt.

Entering her room, I walked over to the bed and looked into her glistening blue eyes. Usually glasses hid this one beautiful thing left about her limp body.

"Mom, the doctor says you can go home on Monday or Tuesday, so I'm going out to try to line up some help, OK?"

"Yes," she nodded while Ann sat beside her bed. I went down the hall to find a pay phone.

"Try Harriet first." Those words echoed in my ear. Harriet turned out to be a remarkable woman who had had thirty years' experience with nursing and death. She usually worked with terminally ill homebound patients. Yes, she said, she was between jobs and available.

"When could you start? What hours could you work?" I asked anxiously.

"Starting Wednesday. From eight in the morning until four in the afternoon," she promised, agreeing to get another aide she knew to help sit with Mom and me throughout the night.

Harriet, always wearing a spiffy white uniform that set off her smooth, chocolate-brown skin, marched into our lives carrying a big leather bag that held her nursing apparatus and her embroidery work. The first day she proved to me she knew how to give sponge baths without hurting, how to turn

Mother over with a sheet with the assistance of only one other person, and how to coax her to take her medicine.

Soon it was almost impossible for Mom to swallow. It was as though her throat was paralyzed. We used a small plastic syringe to pump her pain-killing medicine down her throat one cubic centimeter at a time.

Ann came back to help too. Within a few days, Mom had slipped into a "semi-comatose state," as the visiting health nurse called it.

Four days later was my birthday. Mom was still in a stupor. As soon as the night aide left at 5 A.M., I noticed Mom's eyes pop open. I leaned over and kissed her.

"Mom, I love you. Today's my fiftieth birthday," I continued, talking to her in case she understood. "You remember when Dr. Dody came all the way to Grandma Bailey's old house to deliver me, just as he had delivered you?"

No response. Her eyes stared straight ahead. I waved my hand in front of her face. Still no response.

"Mom, I'm going to say the Lord's Prayer with you again this morning. You just agree with me." I prayed aloud, then repeated Psalm 23 as I always did this time of morning, while I waited for Harriet's shift to begin.

I cranked the rented hospital bed higher to reposition her. "I'll be right back," I reassured her.

Then I flipped on a recording of her favorite choruses and hymns and slipped out of the room to get a cup of coffee. I hummed along with the music.

Just as I reached the kitchen I heard her yell something. "Why, she hasn't said a thing in days," I reminded Ann as we both ran into Mom's room. The song on her recorder was "Open my eyes ... I want to see Jesus."

We watched as through clenched teeth she gave a weak

shout, "Hallelujah! Hallelujah! Hallelujah!" That was all. A faint smile played across her face. Still she showed no recognition of us. Had she heard me talking with her earlier? Had she seen a glimpse of heaven? Then I remembered what the social services nurse had said a few weeks earlier: "I'm sure your mom will say or do something so special you'll always cherish the moment. In fact, you'll be glad you took her home from the hospital."

Her words had stung like tiny balls of hail hurled at my exhaustion. Now I was glad—oh, so glad—she had pushed me, even in my inward pain. I might have missed that special moment to cherish when Mother gave me my best birthday present ever, her last words to me, "Hallelujah! Hallelujah! Hallelujah!"

A few days later, just after Easter, she died in her own bedroom, attended only by Harriet, Ann, and me. I stood at the foot of the bed praying aloud. They each held a hand. After several minutes of gasping breaths, it was over. I could only rejoice. A year and four weeks of fighting this battle was over. The victory was won. A saint had entered heaven.

When I told several close friends when my mother had died, I learned some had at that very moment heard God's gentle voice ask them to pray for her—escorting her in prayer into the heavenlies. Two prayer warriors, Fran and Effie, from Mom's prayer group in Destin, Florida, gathered in a home to pray specifically for her as she was breathing her last. Carol stopped her housework and went to walk on the beach beside the angry wave-tossed surf to intercede for her. Laura, 450 miles away in Melbourne, Florida, put down the manuscript she was writing and walked out onto her screen porch to pray for her. Aunt Betty in California—clear across the States—picked up her Bible and said a special prayer for her.

All this went on at the moment Mom was entering heaven. Oh, the blessedness of intercessory prayer, especially to those of us who feel the loss of a loved one. How comforting to me to learn that God had spoken to each of these women in His quiet way and asked them to stop and pray for my mother.

Time to Relinquish

Sandy Horn, a long-time friend, recently wrote me about her reluctance to relinquish her husband.

I recognized the Holy Spirit's whisper when He told me my husband, Earl, wouldn't be here much longer. But, honestly, I tuned Him out. I didn't want to hear that. We'd been married forty-four years and were raising our teenage grandson, whom we'd officially adopted when he was a baby.

Sixteen years before, Earl had his first heart attack, followed the next year by another. Then he had a stroke that caused him to walk with a bit of a limp but didn't affect his mental abilities or his speech. Each time we went through those medical crises, I had God's assurance that Earl was coming through. I needed him and our grandson needed him, perhaps more.

But on that November day last year when the Holy Spirit told me I wouldn't have him much longer, I didn't want to face the reality that he would leave me. Yet I have come to recognize God's voice.

God had healed me of cancer thirty years earlier—when no one else but me, including Earl, believed He would. But when medical tests showed I had no more signs of cancer even though the affected spots had not been treated with radiation or chemotherapy, it was the catalyst that brought Earl to accept Jesus as his Lord.

I had no inkling that last day in January—less than two months after I'd heard the Holy Spirit's warning—that this was the day for Earl's homegoing to heaven. After shopping we pulled out of the parking lot to head home. All at once he swerved the car. His head swung back against seat. I pulled his foot off the accelerator, pressed my foot on the brake, and stopped the car. A sheriff's deputy was there in two minutes. Two ambulances arrived moments later. But the paramedics could not get his heart started. At the hospital the doctors' efforts also failed.

The months following have been lonely after four decades of marriage. But the Lord has been faithful and I'm still raising our teenage grandson. I don't know what the future holds, but I'm trusting God, who holds my future, and I know it will be good.

Saved at the Last Minute

When Cynthia E. got word that her mother had incurable cancer, she asked the Lord, "Is she going to live or die?" She tells her story:

I didn't hear a word for two and a half years. Finally one day I was praying and waiting on the Lord when He said, *"I want you to pray and fast for your mother's outgoing and incoming."* I knew that He was telling me that she was going to die. For years I had prayed for my mother to become a Christian, but she still had not accepted the Lord.

I began to grieve as though she were already dead. Within fifteen minutes, He showed me a vision. He was standing on the porch of what was my mother's eternal home. Everything was white except for a red carpet that ran from the door of the home down the sidewalk. Jesus was standing with His arms extended.

He told me that, during the next few months, He would be preparing her heart and when the time was right He would send His angels to get her. I knew that He was telling me that the Scripture found in Acts 16:31 ("Believe in the Lord Jesus, and you will be saved—you and your household") was going to come to pass. He had given me this Scripture years ago for my mother.

I came into her room one morning and she said to me, "He came to me."

"He did?"

"Yes. He said that it was a gift."

"It is a gift, Mom. He is the gift. You don't have to work to earn a place in heaven. Mom, if you would only ask Jesus into your heart, you would experience His comfort. He's here to help you." She wouldn't answer. The silence was deafening.

During one of her episodes of intense pain, I said once more, "Mom, if you would just ask Jesus into your heart...."

Instead of silence this time, she gasped and said, "Jesus, come into my heart."

"Ask Him to forgive you for your sins," I coached.

"Forgive me for my sins."

"And take the gift that He told you about," I continued.

"Lord, I take the gift. I take the gift from You. Thank You."

It was an awesome scene. For more than twenty years I'd stood on God's promises that my mother would accept the Lord. Here I was witnessing an answer to that prayer. Two days later, as I was holding her hand, I told her that Jesus was right there with us. It would be an honor and privilege to watch her walk down the aisle, the Bride of Christ, into her Savior's arms. She was afraid, but I told her that if she would look into His eyes, she would see His kindness, His gentleness. She would be with Him, no longer suffering in this world.

She took her last breath with me holding her hand. How glad I was that God had prepared me that she was going to die and not live.

Her Husband's Death

Ruth writes about a significant time when God spoke to her ... on a Sunday in November.

As soon as I finished lunch, I felt a strong impression to go directly to the convalescent center where my husband, Benny, was a patient. The feeling of urgency would not leave me. So I went.

Once I got to his room, I knew I should stay for the rest of the day with him, even skip church in the evening. During the afternoon, several family members came by to visit him. One son, Kevin, came at suppertime and stayed long enough for me to run home to get my husband some Thanksgiving dinner leftovers and some clean clothes.

I did that quickly, again feeling an urgency to return. As Kevin was about to leave, my husband asked me to pray. The three of us joined hands as I prayed, then we all repeated the Lord's Prayer together. Finally Kevin left.

I sat on the bed beside Benny. He put his arm around me and we talked. I had such tender thoughts toward this sweet man who had been through such suffering. His left leg had been amputated just above the knee due to vascular peripheral disease and diabetes. His right foot might soon need amputation as well. His eyesight was also failing. He'd been in the hospital, an acute care facility, and the convalescent center for almost ten months.

Since he had been sitting up most of the day, I imagined he was tired, so I kissed him good night and started home. I pushed in a Christian music tape as I drove off. I'd only gone two blocks when the glory of the Lord filled the car. I turned the tape off and began to sing, "I celebrate my husband's victory. I celebrate Your victory, Lord Jesus—on the cross for all of us." I sang all the way home, making up words as I drove.

I'd just fixed myself a sandwich when the phone rang. A nurse told me that ten minutes after I'd left, my husband had fallen out of bed and hit his head on the floor. Would I meet them in the hospital emergency room?

On the way, the Holy Spirit spoke to me, *"He is already gone."*

Doctors made every effort to revive him. But fifteen minutes later they came to tell me he was gone. There in the hospital I had a quick vision: I saw him running up a hill into the arms of Jesus. That vision was so real to me that as I was getting his clothes ready for burial, I tried to figure out which pair of socks and shoes to put on him. I'd momentarily forgotten he had only one leg and one foot. In my heart I knew he was now whole, in heaven.

The night after his funeral, I was in bed talking to the Lord when He gave me another vision. This time I saw only Benny's head and neck. The Lord spoke to me and said, *"Everything you ever prayed for your husband he has now. He isn't suffering and he isn't grieving anymore. Now you go forward."*

The next morning as I walked across my bedroom to my jewelry box, the Holy Spirit said, *"Till death us do part."* I had not considered that I was no longer Mrs. Benjamin Ward. I stood there shocked, then I heard the Lord whisper, *"The Lord your Maker is your husband. You don't need to put your wedding ring back on."*

When my son walked in, I told him I did not want him to think I was glad Dad was gone, but that I wasn't going to wear my wedding rings anymore.

"Well, Mom," he replied, "at least your marriage ended the way they are supposed to—in death and not in divorce."

How good our God is.

Why My Son?

Beverly had known the Lord since she was twelve. She married, had three children, and saw each of them accept the Lord as Savior too. She shares the loss of one.

My husband and I gave each of our three children to the Lord as soon as they were born. But I always had a fear of losing one of them. I prayed for God to protect them and keep them safe from harm.

On April 29, 1990, at 4 A.M. God answered my prayers in a way I did not expect. Our youngest son, Doug, then twenty-one, was in a head-on car crash. Doug, his friend, and a young man on his way home from his senior prom were all killed. This is where my life-changing journey with God began.

From April to July was a very long three months. I was overcome with many emotions. The one I remember most was anger. I was angry with everyone. Most of my anger was at God. I prayed and He said nothing. I did all I knew to get His attention, but He said nothing.

Doug had spent a lot of his last winter on a ski mountain. I decided if I went up that mountain and got as close to heaven as I could, God would have to answer me. So I did. All the way I was "discussing" things with God.

I was not a nice person and I said things that probably made God put His fingers in His ears. I finally became tired and decided God was not going to answer me, even high on this mountain, so I started down.

I got almost to the bottom, turned, looked up, and trying for the last time cried out, "Why, God, why my son?"

Then I became very quiet and still within my spirit. As I walked on toward the bottom of the hill I heard Him. I had never heard the voice of God sound like it did this time. It was a cry, with the same emotions I had felt when I cried, only much more intense.

"Beverly, why My Son?"

I stopped and looked to see where He was. Then suddenly I was feeling His pain, something I had never thought about. His Son had died too. I knew what Jesus had done for me—how He had suffered for my sins—but I never had thought about what God the Father had done for us that day Jesus died. Or how the Father had felt.

As the days passed I realized God wanted to teach me more. One day God spoke very clearly that He wanted to ask me three questions.

"What was the very first thing you remember after you were told of Doug's death?" He asked me.

I remembered how things turned very dark for me. God said, *"I turned the whole universe dark when My Son died."*

"What do you remember next?"

I remembered how my husband and the sheriff helped me to my chair. I was so shaken I could not stand. God said, *"I caused the whole earth to shake so hard that you will never find a stone that is not cracked."*

He then asked, *"Remember the pain you experienced, which lasts even until this day?"*

I felt the sharp pain that begins at the back of my throat, goes through my heart, lungs, and into my reproductive organs. Then God said, *"As my Son died, He became the sacrifice for all men. I tore the veil in the temple from the top to the bottom so that my children are able to come and talk with Me. To just sit in a quiet place with Me."*

I felt hurt in God's voice as I had felt on the mountain. Then I learned the lesson God the Father had for me. We, His children, do not realize how much we hurt the Father when we don't spend time with Him and talk to Him. Sometimes I would not even talk to Him for days. Then God said something that pierced my heart: *"I not only want My children to talk to Me but I want to talk to them. But they are too busy to listen."*

In this quiet place we can hear Him speak clearly and this is where the healing for all our hurts will come.

These days Beverly stays tuned in to God's voice. She doesn't want to miss it when He speaks. She and her husband comfort other parents when they lose children—in one year eight young people in their local high school died.

Safe in His Care

When Donna, a mother in our next story, suffered a heartache, she learned God's word to her could see her through. She shares her journey:

I could hardly comprehend the news the doctor was giving us about a tumor in our daughter Karin's brain. "It's in the right cerebellum," he explained, "probably infiltrating the brainstem. Doctors can't operate down there. The head of neurosurgery will look at the pictures tomorrow and call me."

Then he looked at Karin and pronounced her death sentence: "You may have only a short time to live."

My husband, John, and I sat there as devastation swept over us. I prayed silently, "There is nothing to say except that we are yours, Lord. Hold us steady."

Twenty-one-year-old Karin had just returned from a year of teaching English in Japan. We knew something was terribly wrong when she walked off the plane, taking tiny steps. John, an oncologist, watched her closely. He gave her a neurology exam and she flunked everything on the right side of her body.

We spent Labor Day waiting for a neurology appointment. It was sheer agony. As I prayed, I felt the Lord tell me, *"Prepare for a long road."*

"But how can I endure this?" I asked the Lord.

"Give her to Me," was His response.

I called my friend Pat and wept. "What should I do, Pat?"

"Only two things help," she said. "Praise and worship God for His awesome power and greatness; then go on with life, Donna. Teach your piano students. Lead your women's group. You may think you have nothing to give, but you will, and they will have a lot to give you."

We shared about Karin's tumor with our church members. They rallied around us. Some prayed with us and shared Scriptures giving us hope and comfort. Others helped us with practical needs such as meals and finding information on disability services. They wept with us, fought alongside us, and helped us hold on to God's truth.

Just before she underwent surgery, the elders of our church came to anoint Karin with oil and pray over her. One began to pray in tongues. When he finished, Karin said, "Don, I know you don't know Japanese, but you just said, 'It's all right. You are safe,' in that language."

The surgery removed as much of the tumor as possible. But the results were not what we hoped for. The tumor had infiltrated the brainstem. We cried when the news came. But Karin was joyful. "I'm alive. I can get up! I can swallow and eat."

As we began the long road of radiation, the church prayer team came weekly to our house to pray. One week as Buddy prayed, he saw Karin "swimming in an ocean toward light, surrounded by light." The Lord continued to tell us in a number of different ways that Karin was safe in His care.

Our family life went on. We vacationed together in the summer. Karin returned to her studies at Ohio State University. But after months of treatment, then a bone marrow transplant, Karin's condition deteriorated. The tumor lodged in her brainstem was still moving on its path of destruction.

Soon Karin was unable to walk. We moved her hospital bed to the dining room. One morning she awoke unable to see and hardly able to move or speak. I struggled with how to pray for healing and prepare for death at the same time.

Our entire family—including our other two daughters and a son—was home now, surrounding Karin with love and care. On Palm Sunday Karin had her "triumphal entry" into heaven. She was finally safe in the arms of God.

In our profound grief, God continued to speak to us and uphold us through His Word and His people. My friend Judy told me, "Donna, you may not be able to run and not be weary, but you can walk and not faint.' She was referring to Isaiah 40:31, about how those who hope in the Lord will renew their strength.

I clung to God's promises, to the things He had spoken to

my heart in my grief: *"I will never leave you or forsake you. I will lift up your hands. I will give you the love of the Bridegroom. I will bind up your wounds. I will be all that you need."*

Donna and others who've shared their stories here discovered that God truly understands our suffering and grief. He walks with us, whether we hear His voice or not. He has promised to be near to the brokenhearted, those crushed in spirit, and to comfort those who mourn.

He will never leave or forsake us—no matter how dark the situation looks and no matter what our losses are.

Prayer

Lord, we throw ourselves on You—for Your mercy to see us through life's losses. We praise You that we don't serve a hopeless God but a victorious Lord. We thank You for Jesus' ultimate sacrifice, for His death on the cross to guarantee our life eternal with You. Amen.

PART 8

God Speaks Protection Over Our Lives

ℰℰ

The Lord is good, a stronghold in the day of trouble, and He knows those who take refuge in Him.

NAHUM 1:7, NASB

The center of God's will is our only safety.

Betsie ten Boom[1]

God revealed Himself to us in the Bible as our stronghold in time of trouble. Ultimately, it is He on whom we must rely as our Protector when confronted with physical infirmity, crisis, natural disaster, political upheaval, or whatever calamity we face.

Sometimes when we need God's protection we have little time to cry more than "Help!" Meet some ordinary people who experienced His protection in their desperate circumstances.

Knowing His Peace in a Crisis

Cheryl was waiting to make a deposit in a bank in Ottawa, Ontario, at ten minutes to eight that Friday night in 1995.

Her husband, Andrew, and baby son waited in the car for her. She wouldn't be long because the bank would close soon. But as Cheryl stood in line suddenly a terrible spirit of uneasiness gripped her. She started praying. What was it? What was wrong?

Then she knew. Two men who had suddenly burst into the bank began making a big commotion with threats and cursings. One spoke to her: "Don't turn around or I will kill you. I have a knife at your back."

She tells more about her experience.

The two men were obviously high on drugs and swore loudly. One waved a gun over us. They wore baseball caps and colored bandannas over their mouths, so we had no idea what they looked like.

I thought about slipping my rings off and placing them in my pocket so the robbers wouldn't take them. As I prayed under my breath, the Lord began to speak to me: *"Don't do that. Just be still."* A sense of God's peace fell over me.

Then the same quiet voice instructed me, *"I am your shield."* A passage popped into my mind. "In Him will I trust ... He is my shield ... my high tower and my strength ... My Savior, thou savest me from violence. I will call upon the name of the Lord who is worthy to be praised, so shall I be saved from my enemies." (See 2 Samuel 22:3, 4, KJV.)

Women around me were crying, some with great sobs. Yet I felt encased in a box of calm. The man with the gun suddenly jumped over the counter to scoop money from one cashier's drawer. As he leaped, his bandanna fell off his face, making it easy to identify him. He quickly moved to the next cashier's drawer, then the next one. Now I thought for sure that we—the witnesses to this crime—might be harmed. We knew what one looked like.

But the men were so bent on getting as much money as they could, they kept on gathering up the cash. When they finished, they ran from the bank, still waving the gun and knife.

My husband, from his vantage point in our car, saw the men when they approached their getaway car. One climbed into the car's trunk, the other jumped in on the passenger side. Then the waiting driver sped toward the freeway to be lost in the heavy weekend traffic. Two months later the robbers were caught because the bank's cameras had snapped a photo of the man who lost his mask as he jumped across the counter.

As for me, I calmly told my husband about God's peace that had encased me. While in the bank, I had never stopped praying under my breath. Miraculously all of us escaped unhurt. Truly God was my shield, my high tower, and my strength. He saved us all from violence.

God Warned Her Before She Reached the Airport

Valerie was in South Africa that summer day of 1997, about to depart for home in Colorado. As friends drove her to the airport in Johannesburg—a drive of several hours—the Lord kept warning her of impending danger.

He told me several times during the ride to be extremely careful at the airport. The words *extremely careful* caught my attention. Then He told me men would be prowling the airport looking for women to rob. The warning was very explicit: women to rob. I asked God for His protection.

When we arrived, the airport was packed with people and their luggage. After only a few minutes, I noticed men, here and there, lurking around the walls—staring at me, following my every move. Again I asked the Lord to protect me. Then I checked in at the desk. When I was told the number of my gate I realized it was a long way off and would take a while to reach.

As I started walking, I noticed the men watching me were now following me. In moments a tall American businessman fell into step beside me. Since we were both from the United States and on the same flight, we starting talking. We had a wonderful discussion about God and life.

I glanced over my shoulder and noticed the strangers who'd followed me were no longer stalking me. I had asked God to protect me and He sent a man from Michigan to escort me to my gate.

Sometimes we listen, like Valerie, to warnings God sends. At other times, like in our next story, we don't even recognize warnings when they come.

Delivered From Troubled Waters

Paula Shields needed God as her Deliverer in her troubled waters. Her very life depended upon Him. She tells her story:

I had gone whitewater rafting before and made plans to go again. Verna, my coadventurer, picked the Kern River near Bakersfield, California. When we met in California, we visited friends of hers. One of them, a nurse, told us several had already died on that river that summer. She begged us not to go out; the river was running very high. High, of course, means more power and more water, but also more danger. We laughed as we told her we were going with an experienced guide, so not to worry.

The next day, at breakfast in a restaurant, we told our waitress what we were doing. She too warned us. "People have lost their lives rafting in that river." Again we laughed.

As we left the restaurant, a man walked over to us and asked what we were doing. When we told him, he too cautioned us that we should not go on the river.

I do not know why we didn't heed the warnings. I know that once I make a decision, I want to follow through with it. And we did, though we made sure we got on the same raft as the head guide for our whole group. After we had maneuvered safely through two sets of rapids, we saw trouble. People on the raft ahead of us had flipped into the water. Our raft—with the head guide—had to lead the rescue. But as we did so, our raft flipped over—and in a very dangerous spot, near trees. Our guides had already alerted us that if anyone fell in the water near these trees, he or she could easily be "sucked down."

And I was! Though I had on a life jacket, I swirled down, down, down, out of control. I was underwater and unable to come up. I am usually very buoyant and can hardly stay under water. What was wrong? Then I realized my left leg was stuck in the tree roots underwater.

I could not move! *I'm going to die—to drown—unless something drastic happens.*

A Bible verse popped into my head: Call on the name of Jesus and you will be saved. I needed to be saved. So I mentally repeated the name of Jesus, over and over. *Jesus, Jesus, Jesus.*

As I did, my leg miraculously came free, and I shot up to the surface, where I still sensed danger. I was being pulled downstream by churning water, and out ahead I could hear the roar of the next rapids—fast approaching. I tried to grab hold of tree branches as I rushed by them. Three broke off in my hands. Finally, a fourth branch held me.

Climbing that branch, I pulled myself out of the current. Holding on for dear life, I turned around to check on the other rafters being rescued. As I waited to be picked up, hoping and praying my branch would hold, I contemplated what I should do. *Praise God in everything,* I thought. *But how do I praise God in this dire situation?* An old Fanny Crosby hymn came to my mind:

> Pass me not O gentle Savior—
> Hear my humble cry!
> While on others Thou art calling,
> Do not pass me by.

I started singing this aloud. Then I just praised God. Finally the raft with the rescuers worked their way toward me, and I was thrown a lifeline.

It takes great courage to let go of the safety of your branch to grab hold of a lifeline. But I did. They pulled me into the raft. I started shaking violently, because I was in shock. When I later tried to walk, I had a limp in my left leg, which had been trapped under that tree.

I learned much through my near brush with death in the turbulent waters. God had tried to warn me three times through people I didn't even know. I ignored the cautions because I wanted to go whitewater rafting, and I was determined to do it. I need to listen more. Now I try to check with Him about everything I do, even fun time.

A year after the incident I heard about an amazing story of intercession on my behalf. At the very moment I was trapped under water, an acquaintance of mine in Holland was praying specifically for me. I came to her mind; she sensed I was in danger and interceded for my safety and protection. I believe her prayers were instrumental in my life being spared. I realize how important it is to respond to those little "nudges" we get from the Holy Spirit to pray. It can be a matter of life and death for someone.[2]

Holy Spirit Prompts Mom to Pray

One mother, many miles away, felt the alert from the Holy Spirit to pray for her grown son.

My son Don has a small engineering firm that does a lot of subcontracting work for large American firms. Because he does one-of-a-kind, special designs that are integrated into power plant monitors, he must often go to faraway places to either repair or reassemble pieces that were disassembled in customs or damaged in shipment.

Just recently he was sent to a country in Asia to reassemble a vibration monitor at a nuclear power plant. He'd been there a week already. Then one morning at 4:00 the Lord woke me up and prompted me to pray for him, especially for his safety. I felt such an urgency in my spirit I got out of bed and went into the den to pray more earnestly for my son's protection. I prayed for some time. Then the burden lifted. Later I called my daughter-in-law to tell her what I had experienced. I just knew Don was in danger.

Several days later she phoned to tell me she'd heard from him. On the way from the power plant to the hotel, the car he was riding in had been hit by a truck. On the same day, I had awakened to pray for him!

Don was twelve time zones away from where I live, but God's timing for intercessory prayer was just in time. Don escaped the accident with minor injuries. What a wonderful Father God we have!

Spared by a Breath of Air

Helene shares how she was spared from danger:

I had been working late one evening. It was the middle of winter and the sun had long ago gone down. I had not eaten and still had work piled up on my desk. I decided to walk across the street to a small restaurant, grab a burger and soda, and then return to my office.

After a quick meal, I headed back across the street to work. I was not really thinking about anything special. A car came along the side of the street. It seemed to pass me by unnoticed. I slowly continued my stride. Then suddenly I heard a powerful command in my right ear, loud and forceful: *"Don't move!!!"*

It took me by such surprise that I abruptly stopped.

Again I heard it, *"Don't move!"*

I froze. As fast as I heard those words, a truck came tearing around the corner, as though the driver was chasing the car. I felt the air blow against me as the vehicle whizzed by, barely missing me. I was wearing a dark winter jacket and I know the driver did not see me. One more step and I would have been hit and probably killed. I know that my life was spared!

Was I thinking about God at the moment? No, not then. But God was thinking about me. Even when we are off in our daily routine, He is with us. I knew when I heard that voice that it was not a human voice but that of God Almighty. How I thank Him for His protection.

Lost in a Crowd of Thousands

God knows when we are lost. This story is not so much one of His protection as it is of His direction. But Sally B. needed both at the time.

Our church group had come to the "Washington for Jesus" meeting in 1986. I, a Florida housewife, was eager to come to our nation's capital to pray for my country. I knew the timing was significant.

But it was raining and a little cold. There was no place to sit, not even on a blanket, as mud puddles were everywhere. I was following my group to a better location when a huge surge of people blocked us off from the ones in front. Those behind me decided to go somewhere else. I was left standing with a

younger woman I did not know. We walked everywhere looking for our group but could not find them.

We stood in the rain holding our umbrellas up and feeling
miserable, a bedraggled pair, wet and cold. Here we were, lost
for the day in the midst of a crowd of thousands, yet wanting
to spend the day with our friends, going where they went,
doing what they did.

I had come to Washington on assignment to pray for my
nation. People were leaving in all directions. Stubborn deter-
mination rose up in me and I thought of people who had it
much worse. What's one day standing out in the cold and rain?

Then I remembered! I know the Lord's leading in my life!
I was standing there forgetting that every day the Lord directs
my steps in little things as well as big.

I looked at the crowd of people and thought, "I'm not an
orphan, lost and afraid. Guide me, Lord."

I told the younger woman to follow me and I started walking. I listened to God's little directions: *"go left."* So I did, past
a group of people huddled together under several umbrellas. I
easily weaved in and out, here and there, on and on past hun-
dreds of people. Whenever I heard *"Now turn right,"* I did.
Then with *"go straight ahead,"* I obeyed. I recognized my
instructions were from the Spirit of the Lord within me.

I raised my eyes to the right, just up a slight incline, and
there they were! We had found our church group. Later that
day, as I thought about it, I realized that, after I had quieted
my spirit, I had experienced the old familiar leadings and urg-
ings of God. His leading came from within and nothing out-
wardly helped me that day. The kingdom of God is within me
and His faithfulness to lead me is always available when I ask.

An Early Morning Fright

As we've seen, protection often comes in following God's direction, as Sally experienced. I, too, had an experience when I desperately needed God's direction. It happened during a period of my life when I felt I should be hospitable to everyone because God said I may even entertain angels unaware. Thankfully He warned me.

It began at 4:30 that morning when our dog, Muffin, kept barking. When LeRoy went outside to check on him, he came back and said, "Couldn't see anything. Probably just barking at a possum or a raccoon." LeRoy continued getting ready for work.

Ours was the only house situated on several acres of piney woods, located at the end of a dead-end dirt road that stopped at the bayou. At 5:00 A.M. I watched from a window as LeRoy drove off for his construction site in nearby Panama City. Day was about to break. As soon as his car was out of sight, I watched, astonished, as two men jumped from behind some bushes and headed toward our front door. When Muffin barked loudly at them, they petted his head until he quieted down.

A friend's son and his fiancée—both college students—were spending the night with us during their spring break. I quickly roused Ward. "Wake up and go to the door. Some strangers are knocking," I told him.

"Don't open the door," a voice urged me. I recognized it as the Holy Spirit's warning. *"Don't dare open up,"* the voice came again. I shared that advice with Ward.

"What do you want?" Ward asked them through the door.

"We want in to use your phone to call a wrecker. Our car is bogged down in the sand about a half a mile up," one said.

"We will call someone to tow you, but you go back to your car and wait," Ward said in his most authoritative voice. As he talked, I stood behind him, praying—for protection, guidance, wisdom.

The men stood on our porch, hesitating, looking our house over thoroughly. Would they try to force their way inside? As I peered through the glass, I could almost see the evil on them. I kept praying. Finally, they turned and walked away. One tossed a beer can behind our azalea bushes, leaving fingerprints. Muffin barked again.

When we called the police department to explain we'd had two suspicious early morning visitors, we learned an incredible story. These two had robbed a convenience store in a town twenty-five miles away, stolen a car, and taken a woman employee hostage at gunpoint. When they stopped for a red light on the main highway a few miles from our house, the kidnapped woman had rolled out of the car and run for help. The men had probably tried to make a getaway on the back sand roads and then bogged down. Both were armed and highly dangerous.

Within a few minutes policemen came roaring with sirens blaring to our house. They talked to Ward and me to get more descriptions and details. "You are lucky, lady, really lucky," they said over and over.

I knew it wasn't luck but God's protection over us. I also knew it was God's provision for my young friend Ward to spend that night with us, for had the men thought I was home alone, I have no doubt they would have tried to force their way in or shot at me through the door. Authorities searched the surrounding woods for several days afterward but never found the men, only the stolen car stuck in the sand.

My natural inclination might be to open the door to

strangers in need, but God had warned me and I had sensed evil.

Staying Sensitive to God's Warnings

God prompts us to do all sorts of things that we don't fully understand at the moment. Later when His promptings unfold, we see the necessity for doing what He told us.

Edith was busy in her kitchen at 9:30 on a Friday morning when a cold chill swept over her. Fear gripped her. *"Dale's in danger,"* a voice warned her. Dale was her married son, an engineer in a manufacturing plant. She stopped to pray for his protection. Five, ten, fifteen minutes, her prayer continued. When she felt all was well, she went back to washing dishes.

That afternoon she called to ask Dale what he was doing at 9:30 that morning. Then she learned why she'd stopped to pray for his safety.

"One of the plant supervisors and I walked out to the plant to go over some plans. A construction crew was remodeling. We'd just stopped to talk when a large steel support beam fell from the ceiling—it hadn't been properly installed. As it fell, one end scraped the arm of the supervisor. If we had been standing even a few inches over, surely the beam would have fallen on us, severely injuring or even killing us," he told her.

He had looked at his watch and he knew it was exactly 9:30. In the natural realm Dale's mom never could have deflected the fall of the steel beam. But because she was sensitive to the voice of the Holy Spirit as she worked in the kitchen that morning, her son's life was spared.[3]

God Even Protects Our Valuables

Sometimes God's hand of protection is not only on our physical bodies but on things we consider precious or valuable. He may use extraordinary ways to accomplish it—as we will see in this next story and in the following chapter.

I was rooming with Ruthie at a Christian conference when she told me how God had protected her property. One night during the church service she heard a voice: *"Your house is being robbed."*

She tried to dismiss the thought. She'd lived in that house for thirty years and there had been no burglaries in her neighborhood. But the more she thought about it, the more it seemed to her that the inner voice she had heard was the Holy Spirit warning her.

"Lord, if our house is being robbed, please send an angel— no, Lord, send a warring angel—to frighten the burglar off." Then she began to quote Scriptures, praying for protection: "No evil will come near our dwelling place.... No weapon formed against us shall prosper...."

Sure enough, when she and her husband arrived home, their back patio door was smashed in and everything inside was in disarray—drawers open and stuff scattered everywhere. The next day, when the police officer came to get a list of the things they knew were missing, all they had to report was one pillow case. He told them that's what a burglar usually takes to stash the valuables.

"As far as we can tell nothing is missing—not even my good gold jewelry," Ruthie told him.

He looked around at her china, silver, gold vases. "With all these beautiful things, I don't understand why you weren't robbed blind. Something obviously frightened away the intruder. He left in a hurry," the policeman said.

Two other houses in her neighborhood were robbed that night. Ruthie is sure God sent a warring angel of protection, as she had prayed and asked Him to do.[4]

Cry Out for Protection

We can say with the psalmist, "In peace I will both lie down and sleep, for You, Lord, alone make me dwell in safety *and* confident trust" (Ps 4:8, AMPLIFIED).

In the midst of our challenges and fears, God is still sovereign. His character never changes. Even in our chaotic world, God really is in control. When Jesus taught us the Lord's Prayer, He said to pray, "Deliver us from evil." I firmly believe our prayers can make a difference in our protection, or in the protection of someone else. As we stay tuned to hear His voice, we may receive warnings or directions, giving us an opportunity to be involved in the safety process.

Betsie ten Boom, who with her sister, Corrie, was imprisoned in Nazi concentration camps for saving Jewish lives, had this perspective. She could say with confidence that "the center of God's will is our only safety."

Prayer

Lord, so many times You have come to my rescue and I have simply neglected to thank You. So often I've had near-accidents, yet I thought it was my own clever thinking that made me escape catastrophe. Forgive me for forgetting that it is You who are my safety! Thank You for the years I've had to live. Thank You for the many ways You've protected me. Amen.

PART 9

Extraordinary Measures: Dreams, Visions, Prophecy, and Angels

ॐ

I will pour out my Spirit on all people. Your sons and daughters will prophesy, your old men will dream dreams, your young men will see visions. Even on my servants, both men and women, I will pour out my Spirit in those days.

JOEL 2:28b-29

How does God turn the ordinary into the extraordinary? Usually by speaking to us in a way we can't fabricate on our own, so only He could be the messenger. Often this requires a touch of the supernatural or using the natural world in a poignant or mystical way. God's acts of communication range from the simple to the sublime, and when we "hear" them, they can change our lives.

Judith Couchman[1]

God has promised to pour out His Spirit on us, so that we will prophesy, dream dreams, and see visions. He didn't stop speaking in supernatural ways when the Bible was finished. Even today He still sends angels as His messengers.

Though some of us have not had visions, prophecies, or angelic intervention, most have had at least one dream that we knew was a direction or a warning. "Scripture indicates a clear linking of dreams, visions, and the prophetic," says my friend Cindy Jacobs, who has a worldwide ministry. "It is not uncommon for God to speak to His people in dreams. Unfortunately, many people ignore most of their dreams or they wait so long to write them down that they forget them."[2]

Sometimes dreams sent from God are to encourage, warn, or direct us. For example, when the apostle Paul needed to know where to preach, God showed him through a dream (see Acts 16:9). Some are just "normal," with no special meaning. Yet others may be symbolic and require us to ponder them, then pray how to interpret them. Some, says Cindy, may have both a physical and a spiritual meaning. Others may be sent by the devil to torment us; we of course want to dismiss these.

A Dream Fulfilled Years Later

The following story tells how one woman fulfilled a dream years after someone dreamed it. She only knew that she heard God and had to obey His instructions.

Dede, an African-American friend of mine, goes to a West Coast city once a year to attend a ministry's board of directors meeting. One year, while there for three weeks of meetings, she dropped into a beauty shop. A young white man shampooed and styled her hair.

As they talked, he told her he had five children; the eldest was ten years old. He was having a hard time getting them to obey. Out of desperation, he had started attending a church. But he admitted to Dede he was truly uninformed about biblical principles to use in rearing his family. Dede suggested that if he read the Bible he'd be more familiar with God's guidelines for a father. She encouraged him to raise his children with a Christian heritage.

"I can't always understand the Bible," he told her. "I will try, though."

As she walked out of the shop after her second visit, she clearly heard God's voice. *"Go buy him a Bible."*

A friend drove her to a Christian bookstore. There she prayed over the variety of Bible translations on the shelf, asking God which one to buy. Finally, she decided on one written in modern English. It included a plan that showed him how he could read it through in one year, by reading just ten minutes a day.

The next afternoon, she walked down to the beauty shop and, when she saw he wasn't busy with a customer, she motioned to him. "Here, I have a present for you," she told him. She had placed the Bible in a bag so she would not embarrass him in front of his coworkers. He didn't open it immediately.

"Step outside a minute, will you?" he asked. "I have something very important to tell you."

Once outside he opened the package. To his surprise and delight, he pulled out the beautiful Bible.

Tears glistened in his eyes. "I didn't know if I would ever see you again. I knew you didn't live here. But I have to tell you this. I was raised in the Catholic church. One night when I was just sixteen I had a dream that a black nun would someday come to see me and talk to me about the Lord. She was wearing a green winter coat and hat—dressed exactly like you. I realized after you left last time that you were the woman in my dream," he said.

"But now it really falls into place—because the black woman also brought me a Bible," he added, patting her arm.

Dede spoke up, "God wanted you to have this Bible. Now you will know the Word of God and can explain it to your children."

"I will read it," he said as he hugged her unashamedly.

A sixteen-year-old boy had a dream. Thirteen years later it came to pass because a woman from two thousand miles away came into his beauty shop and heard the voice of God to go buy him a Bible.

Write a Letter

One woman received direction from the Lord through a dream, after years of frustrating and embarrassing circumstances.

Fanny grew up working in the post office because her father was the postmaster in their little community. When her father finally retired, she was appointed the postmaster by their congressman. It was a prestigious job, though it didn't pay a lot in those days. But Fanny loved serving people.

After a number of years, as the town grew, two clerks were assigned to assist her. Many years passed—uneventful years, really, but full for Fanny, a single mother, who was an encourager to many. She loved her job.

Then one fall after she returned from vacation, her post office was audited. A deposit receipt had been misplaced. The inspector insisted she was responsible. If she didn't resign he said he would bring charges against her. Rather than face disgrace in the town where she had lived all her life, she chose to resign. She knew full well she had not misappropriated any funds. She had done nothing wrong.

Later she realized resigning had been a big mistake. She ended up facing charges and enduring much undeserved harassment and embarrassment. During the years that followed she tried to regain her postmaster's position through her congressman, through legal channels, even through many people writing letters in her behalf. But the federal bureaucracy didn't budge. She finally realized her name might never be cleared.

She worked at odd jobs, some requiring her to stand long hours on her feet in hot, humid weather. She sometimes cooked for restaurants or worked behind a cash register—whatever she could find to do. Then one night she had a dream. She told me, "I was sitting in the post office counting money with my dad, who had long ago passed away. In the dream the count kept coming up short. We counted it several times. Then all of a sudden, the count showed an overage. I felt a presence enter my dream. Though I couldn't identify it, a voice said, *'Write the president.'*"

The next morning Fanny shared the dream with her daughter. "Then, let's do write the president," her daughter responded immediately.

Fanny considered how outrageous that idea seemed. What chance did she have? All other efforts had failed. She had nothing more to lose. Her daughter typed a letter for her to the president of the United States, asking him to intervene so Fanny could be reinstated. They sent it registered mail so someone would have to sign for it and they'd know it had reached the White House.

In the meantime Fanny's daughter shared with a few in her prayer group about the letter's contents and the desire for her mom to be cleared of all charges. They began to intercede for whoever would open the letter. "Lord, let the one who first sees this request be so touched he or she will pass it to the president. Then let him clear Fanny." They prayed this over and over in a period of several days.

A few months later Fanny received an answer to her request and her prayer. Her name was cleared. She could be reinstated in the postal system. The news came from the district office in a nearby state.

By now there were no postmaster openings, so Fanny gladly took a job as a postal clerk. To this day they don't know who actually read the letter. In telling me about it, Fanny said, "I was so happy to be back at work. I thanked God for answered prayer and for speaking to me in such a special and direct way through my dream."

Fanny continued working for the post office until retirement age. She's not one prone to dreams, but she is grateful that, on that night long ago, God chose to speak to her through one. Her obedience led to an amazing answer.

How to Handle Our Dreams

"Dreams are only one source of insight, which must be balanced by what we already know of God and His Word. It would be foolish to make a major decision solely on the basis of a dream. If our dreams urge us in a direction contrary to the laws of God, the laws of the nation, or the basic law of love that should govern us, then we have taken a wrong turn," writes Ann Spangler in her excellent book, *Dreams*.[3]

Sometimes when we have a dream that makes a strong

impression on us, we will want to determine if it is worthy of further consideration. Dreams can be fickle things; some come just from overeating, others from the enemy, to torment us. Here are some steps that might be helpful in understanding your dream:

1. Ask God for more insight on it. "Lord, what does it mean to me? Is it for or about someone else? When do I share it? How will it happen?" He may shed more light while you pray about it. Days later He may bring it back to your memory with more interpretation.
2. Sometimes we need to share the dream with someone whom we trust who has also heard God before in dreams, to confirm our impressions or interpretation.
3. Write it down and add to its interpretation as God reveals.
4. Do something about it. In Fanny's case, she wrote a letter. Other times we are to pray for a person if we dream about him or her.
5. Learn to move when God asks you. Be attentive and obedient to what He shows you. Wait for the right time to share it if you feel you have a warning for someone. Be careful not to move in presumption.

I Saw a Face and I Prayed

One night I saw the face of a woman in my dream, a face encased in fog. No other details, just a face. I recognized her as one of several leaders who had been on the stage with me at a statewide conference where I'd spoken three months earlier. But I couldn't put a first or last name with her face. I woke and prayed for her.

The next night her face appeared to me again. I prayed once more. This went on for several nights. I rummaged through all my past letters, trying to see if I could find a name and address to locate her. Finally, I found a scrap of paper with a scribbled address and wrote telling her I had been praying several times a day for her. Here's her response:

You said that I kept coming to your mind. My, O my! You will understand as I unfold the events of that week. The city where I live is located along the western shores of Lake Michigan with a population of approximately fifty thousand and a dog or two.

On August 6 a storm cell passed over us and stalled. This caused a downpour of over twelve inches of rain in a few hours. Many homes and cars and much personal property were destroyed but no one was killed. The National Guard, Red Cross, and able bodies were busy assisting all.

Our basement flooded with all our belongings there—but we thank God we escaped safely.

Some may think it odd that I would dream about a woman I'd barely met and then pray for her. But I did. I also ask God to put me in the hearts and minds—and maybe the dreams—of those willing to pray for me in a crisis.

Sometimes Dreams Are Warnings

We are all familiar with the biblical accounts of how God spoke to Joseph in dreams—and how he could interpret them, even for a pagan king. In fact, because of his dream interpretations, he was able to help the king save thousands from starving. God warned that seven lean years were coming after seven prosperous years, so they stored up food in advance.

When God speaks to us through a vivid dream, it is sometimes a warning to change our course of action. We may even be spared heartache later on if we hearken to its message. Sometimes the message is warning even for someone else!

I once attended a Christian Prophetic Conference with several thousand in attendance. Two of the leaders there had the same dream on the same night—that an evil man had come to the meeting to sexually entice other men and cause disruption. One of them announced this to the audience that morning. Then he said, "If this man is in the room, we ask you to leave now."

The next day a young man attending the conference was approached in the men's restroom by a strange man who tried to seduce him. He immediately called a security guard, who came and took the man off the premises. It turned out, true to the dream, he had come to seduce other men and to disrupt the meetings.

But God had warned the leaders through dreams beforehand that this intruder was coming and was not willing to receive godly counsel. They had prayed about it together and decided to notify those attending their conference to be on the alert.

Her Dream Brought Her to Repentance

Amanda shared a dream that led to her repentance:

For three years I had been involved in a prayer team ministry, composed of one man, another woman, and me. We prayed two nights a week for two to three hours for people who had deep needs. God set many free from unholy sins and habits as they drew closer to God.

We occasionally brought in other people to train, but they went on to make up their own prayer groups. Our team of three was getting so well known that people came from as far as 150 miles away to be prayed with by our team.

After a while I was aware of the attraction I felt for the man on our team. I'd pray to get rid of my impure thoughts and I'd be OK for a while. Then they would come back. I was repulsed and attracted at the same time. I knew it was wrong, but I enjoyed our wonderful evenings of prayer. I began to prefer being there to being at home with my husband.

Then one spring evening I had the dream. At first I thought it was a nightmare so I rebuked the enemy for disturbing my sleep.

But it was a wake-up call. In my bigger-than-life dream, the man I had developed an attraction for was holding me, ignoring needy people coming for prayer. We were in a church, and he actually asked if he could date me. We walked up to the altar rail. There behind the pulpit on the floor was the Savior, with an agonized look on His face. Mocking devils lurked in the dark around Him.

In an instant, this scene showed me how much Jesus loved me and suffered for me. My heart was broken. He wanted me to have a pure life. I knew I needed to repent, to completely turn away from lustful thoughts at all costs.

The next night when my husband got home from work, he came into the kitchen where I was preparing supper. Very casually he said, "I dreamed last night that you lost your wedding rings."

He never remembers dreams. In our thirty years of marriage he's remembered just three he's shared with me. But if God also sent him a dream, I knew the Lord was trying to get my attention. I was convicted. After supper I went off alone to weep and pray. I knew God was saying, "Break up the prayer team into men praying for men and women praying for women." I told the man I was no longer going to be praying with him, unless some very hard cases came and he brought his wife along. He agreed. Later I learned this turned his marriage around. His wife had felt left out and inferior because she wasn't part of our team.

I was still not happy with my marriage, especially when I compared my quiet husband with other more communicative men. I agreed to go with him to a conference, but one night as I lay beside him in a hotel bed, I found myself praying.

"Lord, please break the sound barrier between my husband and me." I heard one word: *"Amen."* It scared me so badly. I didn't know if it was an angel or Father God. I was profoundly touched by a hope I'd never had before. I knew God was healing my marriage and my heart.

The next year our relationship and love grew as we developed a real bonding. Now I have such a deep affection for him in my heart. The amazing thing is, he doesn't talk more, read less, or watch TV less. He still does those things that used to irritate me.

But I've changed and so have my expectations—by a God who interrupted my life with a wake-up dream. Thank God He gave me the grace to walk out of a potentially dangerous relationship.

Prophecy and Discernment

Prophecy—to foretell under God's divine influence and inspiration, to predict—is a gift God still uses today. In other words, it is God who puts His words in the mouth of the prophet (see Deuteronomy 18:14-19).

Sometimes He gives us a prophetic word ourselves, and sometimes He speaks it through others, as our next story illustrates. Tammy attended a meeting where a well-known Christian prophet was the guest speaker. She came with a very skeptical mind. But she breathed a sigh of relief as she heard him pray, asking God to give him the knowledge he needed as he ministered.

After a while he told her to stand. Then he began to tell her things about herself that he had no natural knowledge about— and he didn't know her. "You like to play sports and coach." That got her attention because she was a physical education major. Then he said something startling: "A member of your family you are concerned about will not die until he comes to know the Lord." She knew he meant her father.

Several months later her father had a severe heart attack. Tammy called him and prayed on the phone with boldness for his complete healing as she remembered the word the Lord had given her through the prophet.

"Dad, you are not going to die. This is not your time," she told him emphatically. Then she prayed silently, thanking God that he would not die until he knew Jesus as his Savior. Doctors were amazed at his immediate and complete recovery.

One day several years later, he went with Tammy to hear her speak at a Christian women's meeting. He waited patiently afterward as several stood in line for her to pray for them. Then he asked his daughter to pray with him to invite Jesus into his life. She was overjoyed at the privilege—and the fulfillment of the prophecy given her years earlier.

Nine years later, he is still well, but now walking with the Lord. Tammy herself no longer doubts God-given words through His prophets today.

Prophecy Encourages Me at a Low Time

I had a personal experience with prophecy that changed not only my thinking about prophets but my life, too. It came from someone I knew.

At a writers' conference in Dallas in the mid-1970s, I got acquainted with a young Texan woman staying in the next room named Elizabeth (Beth) Alves. We stayed up several nights talking nonstop. Exchanging addresses, we agreed to pray for one another.

I soon began to write for Christian magazines and she developed an overseas speaking ministry, primarily in Germany. But all along the Lord was developing and using her prophetic gifts, which I knew nothing about. In fact, I lost track of her when she moved. Then, in 1983, after taking care of my mother for thirteen months while she fought cancer, I needed renewal. I had written little, except to keep a journal of Mom's pilgrimage as she prepared for either healing or heaven.

When she finally went to meet her Lord, I was exhausted physically and spent mentally. Would I ever write again? I didn't feel I had anything left to say or any more writing contacts.

Shortly after her death, I wrote to Mom's prayer partner JoAnne, who now lived in West Germany where her Air Force doctor husband had been transferred. She invited me to visit her and be refreshed in body and spirit. The only decision I had to make was when to go. She mentioned an Aglow women's conference that would be held in October with a speaker named Beth Alves. It had been about nine or ten years since I'd last seen Beth, but I knew in my "knower" that the timing was right for the trip.

What I didn't know was that Beth was staying with JoAnne before the conference. One day after prayer, she said to JoAnne, "I have a word from God for a woman in the States, so pray that I can find her."

When JoAnne asked her who it was, she named my name. JoAnne told her she knew me and I was coming to Germany to attend the conference where Beth would speak. She could save the word and give it to me there. She told her no details of what had been going on in my life.

When I arrived, I rode with JoAnne to the conference center four hours away. I didn't see Beth until she appeared on the platform to speak the first night. Afterward, she called me up before the audience. In essence she said, "The Lord has been working compassion in you these past few months. You will write again. In fact, you will write books that will bless the world. They will even be translated into other languages."

At the time, I didn't know much at all about individual prophecy. I just sobbed, "How, Lord? When, Lord?"

Someone suggested, "If you don't understand God's word at the moment, hide the prophecy in your heart until the Lord brings it to pass. You can't go make it happen."

Six weeks later I attended an Aglow International Conference in Washington, D.C., where a special offering was taken to translate Christian literature into other languages. I prayed, "Lord, not only will I give money to this, but if there is any way You can use my writing talents to have my work translated into other languages, do it."

I went home from the conference, still not knowing God's direction for my writing skills. Two months later I got a call from Aglow's publishing department. "Would you write us a book on how mothers can pray for their children?" the editor asked. She had seen a little booklet I'd written on that subject for a denomination some years earlier.

Finally in 1986 my first official book came out: *How To Pray for Your Children*. It sold more than 100,000 copies in the United States and was translated and distributed in many other countries. Today I still get letters from readers from around the world. I have just finished revising it for another publisher with additional material that includes how to pray for grandchildren.

Since that conference in Germany back in 1983, Beth Alves and I have become close friends. Though we live miles apart, we see each other often, phone, write, and send e-mail messages. Beth is president of Intercessors International and travels the world teaching others how to hear God's voice when they pray.

Weigh Prophecy Carefully and Prayerfully

When someone has a "word" from God for you, you must weigh it carefully. When Beth, who had not seen me in years, got a word from God for me during prayer—though she didn't even know where I was—it was truly God's word for me. How do I know? It came to pass. Cindy Jacobs says, "Certain prophecies need to be prayerfully warred over so that satanic opposition will not keep them from being fulfilled."[4]

The apostle Paul knew this principle and wrote: "This charge I commit to you, son Timothy, according to the prophecies previously made concerning you, that by them you may wage the good warfare, having faith and a good conscience" (1 Tim 1:18-19a, NKJV).

For example, when we have prophecies or promises from the Bible for our children while they are still in rebellion, we may need to do warfare so that Satan won't keep them in his kingdom. One Scripture I find helpful in this instance is: "[God] grant them repentance leading them to a knowledge of the truth, and that they will come to their senses and escape from the trap of the devil, who has taken them captive to do his will" (2 Tim 2:25b-26).

Author Jack Hayford warns Christians to reject any prophecy that does not have a Christ-centered basis. "What place is Jesus Himself given? ... All true prophecy rests in and upon Christ, the Foundation. If that Foundation is soundly built upon, the shape of all that rises will look and sound like Jesus, God's Son."[5] We do need to beware of New Age or other mystical prophecies that do not line up with the Bible.

Visions, the Sense of Sight

Visions are mental pictures we get—much like dreams, but we are fully awake when we experience them.

My friend Cindy Jacobs had lost her passport and had searched fruitlessly for it for days. Finally her husband advised her, "Cindy, calm down and just get quiet before the Lord so you can hear Him."

"When I did this," she says "I immediately had a flash of insight; I knew to look in our tall dresser behind the top left drawer. In a matter of seconds, I had my passport in my hand. God was more likely just waiting for me to ask Him where it was."[6]

Cindy believes there are open visions and inner visions. She had an inner vision when praying about the location of her passport. In her mind she pictured the spot to look. "But an open vision is one where the vision seems as real as anything else going on around you," Cindy writes.[7]

God Used a Vision to Help Her Love

Here's an example of how God spoke through a vision to express His love.

May had just learned her alcoholic father was divorcing her mom after forty-three years of marriage. While attending a retreat she prayed for God to heal her wounds and resentments against her father. As she prayed, she told the Lord she chose to forgive her dad.

Immediately she had a vision of the heavens opening. Jesus, bathed in flames and light, appeared and spoke to her: *"I want to introduce you to My Father."*

In the vision May told the heavenly Father, "I'm sorry, but I don't understand You."

Suddenly she felt inundated with God's love. All the hurts of forty years seemed to wash away as she heard herself saying over and over, "Dad, my dad, he didn't mean to ... he didn't mean to hurt us...."

Shortly afterward, while visiting her elderly father, she told him, "I've forgiven you for all the times you mistreated me. I've been praying for you for years now, and I can say tonight I really love you. I release you from all my judgments and I thank you for what you gave me materially."

Her father's eyes filled with tears as he studied her face and hung onto her words. Before the week was over he called

May's sister for the first time in twenty-five years and talked for an hour. He ended the conversation by saying those three wonderful words, "I love you."[8]

A Vision of Biscuits and Blessings

Perry tells how God encouraged him not to give up—through a vision.

Monday night my wife became very ill. It came on the heels of weeks of financial struggle in our business. It hit me hard. We just didn't seem to be getting ahead of the game. I felt helpless.

I went outside to "yell" at God for a while. Though I don't recommend yelling at God, I don't believe it is wrong to strongly plead our case and call upon the Lord to come to our rescue. I hope that was how He interpreted my frustration.

After I got it all off my chest, I went back to bed and began to pray. As I did, God gave me a vision—it must have been a vision, because I wasn't sleeping.

I saw a table with just one biscuit on it. I knew this was my biscuit. Next I saw someone come take a large bite off the top, leaving me the crumbs. It struck me as odd at the time. Then I heard the Lord say, *"It's OK, Perry, I have plenty more biscuits for you to enjoy and enough to distribute."*

Then in the vision, I saw just a glimpse of a pan full of browned biscuits, fresh from the oven. I sensed there were plenty more to come, but not just yet.

Waiting for the next pan of biscuits or sheet of cookies is where many of us find ourselves today. I certainly do. But I know if I just hang in there, the baking is almost over and the blessing and distribution is coming very soon.

Not long after this vision my wife's condition improved and so did our business finances. So you could say I'm getting more than crumbs right now.

Angels Today?

Sometimes God sends angels as encouragement to us—those supernatural beings who, according to Billy Graham, "are God's messengers whose chief business is to carry out His orders in the world."[9] They also protect His children. Angels or "messengers" appear dozens of times in the Bible. (See Part 12 for more examples.)

People who've never had an angel visitation might be skeptical. I've never seen one myself, but our fourteen-year-old daughter saw a whole choir of them in our church's loft during a Sunday evening worship service. Afterward she described their beauty and music to her father and our pastor and explained how God used them to encourage her.

On another occasion, when my mother was on the oncology floor of the hospital, a friend offered to stay with her while I went down to the cafeteria to grab a hot lunch. When I returned Mary Helen told me she'd watched two massive angels standing guard over Mom's bed, one at the head and the other at the foot, the entire time I'd been gone. What comfort it brought me, though I didn't see into the supernatural myself.

I have made it a habit to ask God to station angels around my car whenever I put my key into the ignition. Once, when an elderly man crashed into my car, totally wrecking it, I surprised the first fireman to get to me. He asked where I was hurting most.

As I held my head, which took the hardest blow, I managed to say to him, "I'd just prayed for God to send an angel to protect me before I drove out of that parking lot."

"You probably had more than one angel to spare your life," he said, assessing the damage and my superficial wounds.

Sit down and think about times God has spoken to you in a supernatural way or answered a prayer in an extraordinary manner. You may be amazed! Next time you have a dream, a vision, or a prophecy, don't fail to see if God is trying to speak. Keep a notebook of what and how God speaks to you personally.

Prayer

Lord, thank You for speaking to us, even today, through dreams, visions, and prophecy. I rejoice in the times You send an angel as Your own special messenger. Help me not to dismiss the ways that You want to speak to me, just because they are not the norm for me. Thank You that Your Word gives me encouragement in accepting these different ways. Amen.

> For God does speak—now one way, now another— though man may not perceive it. In a dream, in a vision of the night, when deep sleep falls on men as they slumber in their beds, he may speak in their ears....
>
> Job 33:14-16a

PART 10

God Speaks His Love Through Others

૪ৈ

Dear friends, let us love one another, for love comes from God. Everyone who loves has been born of God and knows God. Whoever does not love does not know God, because God is love. This is how God showed his love among us: He sent his one and only Son into the world that we might live through him.

1 JOHN 4:7-9

Whether you are blessed with soul mates who settle into the most comfortable room inside you, or with those who walk with you just a little while, not one of these people crosses your path by chance. Each is a messenger, sent by God, to give you the wisdom, companionship, comfort, or challenge you need for a particular leg of your spiritual journey.

Traci Mullins[1]

One sure way we can know we are hearing God is to express His love by reaching out to others—sometimes even those we don't know.

This can take the form of a letter written at a critical time in a friend's life, a timely phone call, a greeting card of encouragement, a meal delivered when things at home are in turmoil, or even prayer offered. How simple but life-touching these things are!

One afternoon my friend Bobbye found herself reaching out to a stranger in the grocery store. Twice she'd caught herself staring at the young woman, an extremely attractive, petite blond. She had thought, "Lord, You have such good taste to create someone so beautiful. But she is troubled."

The third time her eyes locked with the young woman, they were both standing in the checkout line. Bobbye said, "God drew my attention to you—I'm sorry I was staring." Tears spurted from the woman's eyes. Bobbye knew she had hit a tender spot. "Could we talk after we've paid for our groceries?" Bobbye asked.

"Yes, of course."

As soon as they were outside, they went to Bobbye's car.

"Do you know the Lord?" Bobbye asked.

"I used to," she said, "and when you said God drew me to your attention, I knew He hadn't forgotten me."

She continued with her story. "I started crying because I'm about to be married, but today the doctors told me I have cervical cancer—the test results from my premarital exams were back."

Bobbye, a woman of faith and prayer, asked if she could pray for her complete healing. She nodded in agreement. Bobbye prayed for the Lord to heal her body and soul. They exchanged names and phone numbers; two weeks later the young woman called her at home with good news. She was cancer free. As the two of them had prayed in Bobbye's car that afternoon, she'd received a physical healing—and an emotional one too.

She went ahead with her wedding plans. She made a recommitment to the Lord and continued to get teaching and prayer as she met Bobbye at Christian women's meetings for some time afterward.

A chance encounter in a grocery store? I don't think so. I believe it was a divine setup. Bobbye, in the right place at the right time, was sensitive to His Spirit to reach out to a young woman who, in a tender place, was ready to respond to His wooing her. A beautiful healing resulted.

God Is Looking for Ambassadors

My pastor, Dutch Sheets, writes in *Intercessory Prayer:*

There are many wounded and hurting individuals around the world. You work with some, others live across the street. One of them probably just served you in a check-out line, seated you in a restaurant or served you food. Their chains are alcohol, drugs, abuse, broken dreams, rejection, money, lust....

Plan A is for supernatural, but ordinary people like you and me to (1) wholeheartedly believe in the victory of Calvary ... and (2) to rise up in our role as sent ones, ambassadors, authorized representatives of the Victor. Our challenge is not so much to liberate as to believe in the Liberator—to heal as to believe in the Healer. Plan B is to waste the Cross; to leave the tormented in their torment; to scream with our silence: "There is no hope"; to hear the Father say again, "I looked, but found no one."[2]

Mrs. Buttons Sews

Maebeth Cruse is a grandmother who had no clue God could use her as His ambassador in a far-off country. In fact, she thought she had no special talents to share until God spoke to her. She told me her story:

I'd been taking a class on finding your niche in life. But I hadn't been able to define mine. After class one night when I was most discouraged, I cried as I drove home and prayed, "Lord, isn't there something I can do without pay that would help others and please You? Show me. Please show me." I cried again. I could think of nothing.

But when I walked into my living room, He clearly said, *"Here it is."*

Hanging on racks were children's clothes that had been there for two years. My friend and I had made them but we hadn't known how to market handmade things, so we had just stored them—in my living room. Now that my eyes were opened to see them, again I had questions.

"How, Lord? What do you mean? I see the clothes."

Quickly He brought to mind a newsletter I'd read two weeks earlier at the ministry where I work. The director for an orphanage in India had written asking for Christians to come and shower love on the twenty-one children there. I couldn't quit my job and go for even a short-term mission, so I'd dismissed the plea.

But now, this moment, God pulled one sentence from the letter and brought it to my heart: "The children came here with nothing but the clothes on their backs." Now I saw it. Their clothes were on my racks. I did have a mission, a talent. I'd been sewing since I was little. At one time I had even designed costumes for dinner theaters in New York. God had been preparing me all these years through a talent I never thought was that special.

Then I remembered when I was eight years old and not living with my parents. Someone gave me a new Christmas dress with thirty-five tiny buttons on it. Every time I wore it I felt special, remembered by someone who cared enough to touch my life.

I decided to call my ministry of making clothes for the children simply "Mrs. Buttons." On the inside of every dress or outfit, I decided to sew a bright little button in a hidden place with instructions for the children to find it. When they saw or felt the button they would know that someone was praying for them.

Who would have thought God would use me, my ability to make clothes, and even use tiny buttons to reach children halfway around the world? I've found my niche.

Today, several years later, Maebeth is still making clothes for the little girls in her after-work hours. She buys T-shirts and shorts for the boys instead of making them, but they too get a special button sewn into their clothes. Three people now help Maebeth to sew on the buttons. Others also help her buy school uniforms for the youngsters.

Barbara's Two-Minute Encounter

Barbara James believes God arranges our personal encounters when we specifically ask Him. She calls this her "two-minute" miracle encounter.

She had signed up to attend a conference in North Carolina related to her work. She writes: "Because I did not know anyone who would attend, I prayed earnestly that God would order everything down to the smallest detail during that week—every contact, every conversation, every point of communication—according to His divine purpose. Then I went to the conference.

"On the way to the auditorium one day I met a woman named Dot on the sidewalk. Briefly we exchanged names, addresses, and other information. I added Dot's name to our monthly prayergram."

Five years later Barbara received a surprise phone call from Dot inviting her to come teach at a large retreat in her state. While there, Barbara discovered another unique piece to her miracle puzzle. Dot had attended the North Carolina conference five years earlier because a friend of hers felt God wanted her to sell a rug to pay for Dot's registration.

"How awesome are the ways of God," says Barbara. "If that one woman had failed to hear and obey, Dot would never have attended the conference. If my own heart had not been stirred to ask God to order every contact, I might have missed a two-minute conversation that resulted in a phone call five years later to go teach many women."

Barbara would also have missed out on a friendship with Dot that continues some twelve years later, as well as other speaking invitations she received as a result of that retreat.

"Imagine, all along God knew!" Barbara concludes. "He kept track! He fulfilled His holy purpose. An appointed time, appointed place, person, and ministry, all of which evolved around a two-minute encounter. When we are yielded to God, trusting Him to 'redeem the time' in our lives, that grace carries awesome, long-term potential. God not only gave me the two minutes, He watched over it until the season for its fullness."

That, I think, is the essence of her divine appointment—God's season for fulfillment! How hard it is not to get impatient when things don't go our way, in our timing. But God knows the how and why of each little detail of our lives.

Just Make a Pot of Stew

One day Louise woke up "burdened" to make a pot of stew and take it around the corner to a certain neighbor, even though she hadn't been in contact with the neighbor in a long time.

"Somehow I was impressed to cook it," Louise remembers, "then to deliver it at an exact moment. When I arrived, I discovered my neighbor was just being brought home from the hospital and needed a hot, cooked meal."

These nudgings from God are His way of speaking to us to

bless others. How many times we miss them! Louise puts it well: "God's ways are simple. I discover Him in the ordinary of my life."

Longing to Make Her Special Fudge

God speaks His love, I believe, when He answers our prayers—even those we may think are insignificant or too small to bother Him with.

Just ask Treva. Last Christmas she brought me a plate of the most delicious chocolate fudge. When I asked about the recipe she told me her story. Treva always made chocolate fudge at Christmastime. She couldn't remember a Christmas when she hadn't, not since the day her dad passed his recipe on to her. She still did it, she thought, sort of as a remembrance of him. But she always shared it with her friends too.

One year money was especially tight. Her husband was dying of diabetes, and Christmas looked dreary indeed. Treva was accustomed to talking to the Lord about every need she had, especially during the long months she'd nursed her sick husband. Now, as the holidays approached, she knew her desire to make fudge was not necessarily a need, but she spoke about it aloud.

"I'd really like to make that chocolate fudge recipe that's my Christmas special. But, Lord, you know I don't have the money to buy the ingredients. It will be the first Christmas in my life when I won't have any."

She had hardly voiced her prayer when her friend Joy called from church. "We're bringing you over some groceries," she announced.

As Treva unloaded the sacks, she was excited to find a turkey with all the trimmings to cook for a traditional holiday dinner. Then she realized her friend had brought her all the necessary ingredients for her fudge—except for pecans.

"By the way, Shirley sent these over to you," Joy said, handing her another bag. Inside were five pounds of shelled pecans.

Tears of joy sprang from Treva's eyes. She recalls, "I really knew God loved me to care that I had fudge for Christmas when everything else seemed so bleak. I could carry on the family tradition of making it and enjoying sharing it."

Every Christmas after that Joy brought Treva the ingredients for her delicious fudge, until the year she remarried and could buy it herself.

Joan's Extra Room

Sometimes after we've experienced a touch of love from God, He wants us to pass it on. Reaching out to others with His love doesn't always come at a convenient time or to the most lovable people.

Soon after her son moved out of his basement bedroom, Joan prayed, "Lord, use me and use this room to your glory."

Two days later she got a letter from a woman she'd known years before, written from a "safe house" in another city. Did Joan know anyone who would take her in and let her start life over? Recuperating from an abusive relationship, emotionally and mentally spent, she needed help.

Joan prayed, "Lord, this will be a big responsibility—am I to do it?" Walking across her front lawn she weighed all the pros and cons of taking in such a needy person. Then, she says, the Lord clearly whispered, *"As I've extended grace to you, you extend grace to her."*

Extend grace! Joan, a single mom who had raised her son alone while running a home-based business, knew how much grace God had given her. Yes, she would try. And she did.

But the woman brought with her lots of emotional baggage and some stubborn ways. Joan's patience was tried beyond what she could have imagined when she said yes to God's request. Daily she depended on God to expand her heart to share His love with her houseguest.

When we know God we let His love flow through us to touch others. 1 John 2:3 says, "We know that we have come to know him if we obey his commands." That "know" means that we see God in action; we are aware that it is God with an absolute certainty.

Corrie and the Chess Game

How surprised we are sometimes when we discover a special kindness was extended to us and we weren't even aware of it. That's what happened to an American doctor and his friend, Dutch evangelist-writer Corrie ten Boom.

Corrie had led Dr. Mike Ewing and his wife, Frances, to the Lord. During their sixteen years of friendship, she spent many of her working vacations with them, whether they lived in Virginia, Georgia, or Florida. Eight of those years Corrie's nurse-companion Ellen de Kroon joined her at the Ewing home.

After Corrie put in eight hours of work—writing her books

and answering her mail—with a lunch break and a ten-minute nap sandwiched in between, she'd go hunt down Mike. "How about a game of chess?" she would ask him.

Mike believed Corrie liked to play chess to unwind after being on the road speaking and as an opportunity to spend quiet time with a trusted friend. Corrie, on the other hand, used Mike's interest in chess as a way to encourage him to talk.

"I'm writing a chapter on suffering, Mike. What do you think the purpose of suffering is?" she'd ask.

"Oh, I don't know that much about suffering," he'd say, evading her.

Actually both had suffered much: Corrie in a Nazi prison for hiding Jews in her home during World War II; Mike when polio left him paralyzed when he was just thirty-two and a doctor in the U.S. Army. He learned to play chess while in therapy at Warm Springs, Georgia, and never played again until Corrie came along.

Corrie was old enough to be Mike's mother, but she didn't want to be treated like "a double old grandmother," as someone once called her. Mike, every bit the independent-thinking intellectual, would sit for hours in the evenings listening to Corrie share about the Bible—while they played chess.

At first Mike won nearly every game. Finally he asked Fran to pray with him that God would handicap him in his chess game because he knew Corrie was too smart for him to let her deliberately win. Almost immediately, to Corrie's delight, they began swapping wins, game for game. "Mike, I like to play chess with you better than anyone in the world, because we are exactly the same," she told him.

In time her health deteriorated. She had a pacemaker

implanted to regulate her heart. Then she had a stroke and was confined to her bed in California. Ellen in the meantime married a university chaplain and they had two youngsters. One fall she wrote Fran and Mike, asking if she and her family could visit them at their Florida home.

One afternoon, soon after they arrived, the Ewings took Ellen and her toddlers to play along the beach on the Gulf of Mexico. As Fran and Ellen talked, they began to reminisce about Corrie.

"How I miss her!" Fran sighed. "Ellen, it doesn't seem right for her not to be here with you, with us. Remember how Corrie loved to play chess with Mike? She'd beg for just one more game. Mike wasn't really that enthusiastic about playing chess. He played only to please her."

"To please her—Corrie?" Ellen said with surprise. "Frances, Corrie didn't play so much chess with Mike just because she liked the game!"

"Really?" Fran answered, a bit puzzled.

"God told Corrie years ago to try to draw Mike out of himself. Chess was just one way she could do it. In the early years, you know he kept his personal thoughts and feelings to himself. Sitting across the chessboard gave her an opportunity to get Mike to talk and to share biblical truths."

Fran couldn't believe it. Corrie and Mike, who had played chess together for almost sixteen years, had done it each for the other. Mike and Fran had prayed for God to handicap him so that Corrie would have fun playing. Corrie had prayed and played so she could get Mike to come out of his shell.

Both prayers were wonderfully answered. While Corrie and Mike were moving chess pieces on their board, God was moving Mike and Fran into positions where He could use them to teach Bible studies. They've been doing it for years now.

The chess game Mike and Corrie played was a game in which Jesus was clearly victor.[3]

Corrie was born in Holland in 1892 and died April 15, 1983, on her ninety-first birthday. She had her framed tapestry, "Jesus Is Victor," sent to Mike after her death. Mike, now in his seventies, still gets around in his wheelchair. Today his favorite chess opponent is his thirteen-year-old grandson, Joshua.

Love Because Jesus Said to Do It

I firmly believe God brings people into our lives by divine appointment, often so His destiny for us can be accomplished. Some of these people are pure serendipities—friendship pleasures that money couldn't buy.

"Just get busy ministering in His name and in His power," suggests pastor Jack Hayford. "But don't do it to be seen and appreciated by others; do it just for Him."[4]

Prayer

Lord, thank You for special people You bring into our lives. Some for us to love for You. Others to love us because of You. What blessings they are. Thank You that You said that "whatever you did for one of the least of these brothers of mine, you did for me" (Mt 25:40). Help us to be more sensitive to love others and to reach out in Your name. Lord, make my ears hear what You want me to hear! I pray in Jesus' Name. Amen.

PART 11

Listening for God Anytime, Anywhere, Anyhow!

❧

But which of them has stood in the council of the Lord to see or to hear his word? Who has listened and heard his word?

JEREMIAH 23:18

As the Lover of my soul and yours, He wants to be close, to disclose Himself to us, and yes, to speak with us, for our ears alone....

The Lord is wanting to say something to you now—at your age, where you are this week, this day, this period in your life.... Are you seeking His voice?

Jack Hayford[1]

God can speak to us anytime, anywhere, anyhow, or any way He chooses. Doesn't it just overwhelm you that the God of the universe wants us to keep our ears open to hear Him always?

Just as we learned to walk as babies, we grow in our listening skills as we mature in the Christian faith. We also become grateful when we realize He does speak—and not just when we cry out during times of trial.

The shepherds, you remember, were having an ordinary night in their field outside of Bethlehem, just watching over their sheep. Suddenly an angel appeared to tell them good news: Christ the Lord, our expected Lamb of God, had been born in a stable. At first they were terrified, but the angel commanded them not to be afraid. *Suddenly* is a word that appears twice in this Christmas passage.

The Bible is full of unusual ways God speaks. But He hasn't stopped.

He Speaks Through Nature and Music

Sometimes our Creator uses nature to communicate with us— when we take a walk through the woods, a stroll on the beach, rock in a boat on a lake, or watch a thousand snowflakes fall outside our window. He speaks to others in solitude, during complete silence. Still others set aside times to fast in order to hear Him more clearly. Some of us, myself included, like to hear Him while soaking in the tub or enjoying an invigorating shower.

Those who relate well to music may hear God's voice as a message through a song that plays over and over in their thoughts. Some hear Him as they listen to worship music, the words of the song penetrating deep within their spirit with a special directive from God. Who hasn't thrilled at Henry Van

Dyke's hymn "Joyful, Joyful, We Adore Thee," which calls us to look at nature to praise God?

> Field and forest, vale and mountain,
> Flowery meadow, flashing sea,
> Chanting bird and flowing fountain,
> Call us to rejoice in Thee.

For the visually attuned, God may use pictures or visions. My friend Tommi Femrite wrote of her experience:

> On a recent trip to Europe, I went for a long walk in the hills of Switzerland to be alone with the Lord. I was taken by the loveliness of the flowers. Buttercups one inch in size. Dandelions about two inches wide. Trees were dripping with apple and cherry blossoms. Lilacs and spirea were ready to burst forth. The fragrance was delicious. Other flowers cascaded down the walls on the side of the road. I continued to walk through the vineyards and then the woods, finally coming out in an open field where I could look out over the city of Winterhur with the Swiss Alps in the background.
>
> Standing in awe of God's spectacular creation, I opened my mouth to speak praises to the Lord. Suddenly, I found myself singing at the top of my lungs. I sang for some time about God's loveliness and how my soul longs for His presence. "My heart sings for joy to the living God.... You are my King and my God...."[2]

The Lord spoke to her through His creation about His loveliness, His goodness, His beauty. On nature walks we can experience a deep intimacy with God. It's not unusual to begin to express to Him our worship and praise—out loud. While God longs for our fellowship, in solitary walks with Him we can encounter it.

God Speaks Through Art

I had known that God uses our senses of sight, touch, smell, and hearing or any level of our being to speak to us, if we let Him. But it took a significant event and a painting to turn that "knowing" into real experience.

Rembrandt's *The Prodigal* is just one of more than two million works of art exhibited in the Hermitage in Saint Petersburg, Russia. About twenty of us were following our tour guide as she chose what she considered the most important ones for us to see.

When we came to *The Prodigal* several of us were so awestruck by its powerful message that we asked the guide to let us stay and meditate on it while she took the group on to view other magnificent works. Three of us remained glued to our spot to study it.

The Dutch painter Rembrandt had been one of the most significant artists in the seventeenth century. Yet at that moment his work was not just a three-hundred-year-old painting, but rather a reassuring message from God to me. Tears clouded my vision as I studied it.

"I love you even more than this father who is welcoming home his beloved son who was lost," God spoke to my heart. *"I long to welcome home so many more of my prodigals."* Standing there I sensed a new commission, a new call to pray even more for those who don't know God as their loving heavenly Father.

Soon another tour group crowded around to view the painting. Their guide pointed out the dark colors, the soberness of the scene. Her explanation pierced my heart.

"This painting is a scene of a man and his son that is just a myth, a fable," she assured them.

More tears splashed down my cheeks. In truth Rembrandt's painting depicted a story Jesus himself shared with his disciples: a son who took his inheritance and spent it on wrongful living makes a decision to leave the pigpen and go home to his father and ask his forgiveness. His father joyfully welcomes him, bestows on him the best robe, and puts a ring on his hand and shoes on his feet. Then he sets a magnificent banquet for him. Jesus gave us the story to show how much our heavenly Father loves us and rejoices when we choose to come to Him (see Luke 15:11-32).

"God, let Your truth be revealed to those who from this moment on view this painting. Unveil their eyes that they may see Your overwhelming love," I prayed.

She Learned to Hear Him in a Grocery Store

We don't have to go to an art museum to hear Him. He speaks even during our ordinary tasks in life. God trained one woman to hear Him in a place most of us women go frequently.

When I look at how God has trained me to hear Him, I laugh and say it was in the grocery store. With four kids and lean finances in the early years, I had to go often and watch carefully how I spent the money. Well, the Holy Spirit would simply turn my eyes to something as I was walking down the aisle and I would "know" I should get that ketchup. I'd get home, and sure enough, we'd be almost out. The times I ignored these impressions and used my natural reasoning and memory, invariably I'd return home to realize it had been the Lord speaking to me in the grocery store.

Often He tells me how many of something to buy. Many times, I've stood in an aisle and said, "I can't remember what I need," and His presence has come to help.

It was in the grocery store that I learned how to receive the gentle impressions and go with them, that it was God's voice whispering to me.

He Even Speaks Through Newspapers

Sometimes God speaks through ordinary events. When you ask Him to guide your steps and guard your thoughts, you can count on Him to give you answers to decisions in the routine things of life.

One day when Loretta considered getting a loan against her house to deduct taxes and interest, she thought, "What a wonderful idea." But the next morning she read an article in the newspaper that warned that the fastest way to lose your house is to take on a second mortgage. "God was speaking to me and I did not get a loan," she wrote me. How glad she is now, years later, that she obeyed that prompting.

Maybe you think it is amazing or impossible that we can get a spiritual insight from reading the newspaper. But God can speak to us any way He wants, at any time.

Not long ago, Ann Landers published a letter from a successful artist who said that when she attended her fiftieth class reunion, she learned her high school art teacher was still alive. She wrote her a letter to thank her long-ago teacher and to let her know how much her encouragement had meant to her and how art had enriched her life.

The teacher answered back, saying she was aware of her student's success, but in all the years she had taught, this was the first pupil to write and thank her.[3]

The Lord pierced my heart with that letter. How many people had I written to thank for their encouragement to me over the years? How many notes of appreciation had I sent to writing mentors? Spiritual moms? People who had prayed for me? Pastors who had believed in me when I needed it most?

I stopped everything and wrote five letters of thanks that day, simply because I believe God spoke to me through a little 150-word article in a newspaper.

Pecking and Bad Habits

Liz was annoyed when her favorite tree was attacked. But God used the incident to speak to her heart.

At first I was amused at the daily tap-tapping of that red-headed woodpecker. Then I was annoyed as he spent the summer pecking holes in my queen palm. I had planted it twenty-four years earlier and had watched as it grew from three feet tall to more than thirty.

Tall and graceful, it made a lovely silhouette of dancing fronds against the blazing Florida sunsets. Now it was gone! Crashing across the yard during a storm, it lay there as if torn on the dotted line. As indeed it had. That woodpecker had completed a circle of large holes around the circumference of the tree. A strong gust of wind had snapped it like a twig.

Standing amid the debris, I heard the Holy Spirit whisper this message to my heart: *If a tree that large can be felled by a bird that small, think of the damage small negative habits can do in your life. Like the continual tapping of the woodpecker, a negative habit can slowly open your life to destructive forces."*

I stopped and prayed, "Lord, show me how to guard my heart. Bad habits seem to come so easily and go so slowly. Help me develop positive ones."

Stop the Caffeine Habit

Lynn had a habit God wanted to deal with. She loved coffee as much as she did sunsets. She wasn't about to give up either one. No matter that coffee gave her such bad breath that her children refused her hugs or that she had the shakes all day from drinking too much.

One night when Lynn was in prayer, the Lord seemed to say, *"Tomorrow you are going to stop drinking coffee."* She spent the next thirty minutes telling Him she simply wasn't willing to give it up.

The next day as soon as she woke, Lynn heard a little voice say, *"Today you are giving up coffee."* She knew that, if she did, the Lord would have to do a miracle to keep her from desiring it. She told Him so!

She went into the kitchen, rummaged around until she found an old tea bag in the cupboard, and made herself a cup of tea. Her husband soon joined her in the kitchen and started brewing a pot of coffee. Though Lynn is confident it must have produced a savory aroma, this time she couldn't smell it.

To this day, some fifteen years later, when coffee is brewing, Lynn's sense of smell is oblivious to it. She says, "When I can't smell it, I don't desire it. Since the day I gave it up, I have never yet been able to smell it brewing."

You may say that's a funny coincidence. But Lynn will tell

you it is a miracle for two reasons. First, God told her to do it for her own health. Second, He made it easy. And her three kids love to give her hugs now!

Holy Spirit Convicts Her of Pride

We don't always like to admit we are blind in some area of our lives, but one way God's Spirit speaks to us is to convict us of sin (see John 16:8, NASB). Angela tells me she is a perfect example of this.

As head intercessor in her church, Angela was privy to lots of information the pastors shared with her to take to her prayer closet. Then one day during a service, the pastor announced to the congregation a new name for the church and new staff members.

Angela hadn't been told about the change. She went flying to the bathroom, angry. But she knew she had to seek God's voice. "Lord, I don't understand. They didn't tell me in advance. This has caught me off guard. I'm hurt."

"What makes you think you have to know everything that goes on around here?" God spoke to her heart.

She fell on her face, sobbing, asking Him to forgive her. Later she told me, "Since that day on the floor before God, I have not had any desire to know what's going on at the church. God dealt with my pride. I'm still the intercessor but it doesn't matter whether I have any facts or not. God changed my heart when I asked Him to forgive me that day in the bathroom."

God's Housecleaning Business

Another woman wrote about God's housecleaning in her heart. Dora says she seems to be more certain the Lord has spoken to her when she is most jolted by what He says.

I do not diminish the stirring of my heart and enlightenment of my understanding that often comes as I listen to a sermon, interact in a Bible study, or sit in His presence, journal in hand. But when He surprises me, I come up for air saying, "I would never have thought of that."

Shortly after our daughter moved to New York, I spent a few days with her. She was in the process of finding a home church. This particular week we visited a small congregation where the pastor was recruiting volunteers to clean the home of two elderly women. The health department was moving them out. I sat there thinking, "While my daughter's busy during the day, I could help with that."

The pastor was shocked by my offer. "My wife's a nurse and I know she couldn't take it," he told me.

The next morning I saw why: dead mice and rats under piles of newspapers, sickening smells, filth everywhere. One of the women had already been removed. The other sat numbly by in an easy chair, seemingly oblivious to the work going on around her. I lasted three or four hours at the most.

A few days later, back in my own home, I asked the Lord, "What was that all about—a lesson in servanthood or what?"

"No," He answered. "I was giving you a picture of what I am doing in your life."

Oh, the brokenness! Immediately I saw myself as that invalid woman. I could not help myself. I could not even see what needed to be done. As strange as it might seem, I did not receive that word as a harsh one. If anything, I came away knowing more about the love of the Father, who goes to whatever length necessary to get His message across. All I could do was respond, "Lord Jesus, I give You permission to do Your work in me."

The Holy Spirit Draws Us to Jesus

Because the Holy Spirit is the One who woos us, convicts us, and guides us to accept Jesus, He may speak to us before we are even Christians.

Reared in a cultlike religion, Debbie was taught only that Jesus was a good man. She had little understanding about the Holy Spirit or Father God. Then one day she went to a Christian meeting with friends.

After listening to lively music and interesting preaching, she clearly heard a still small voice. She recognized it as holy: *"Debbie, I want you!"*

"Yes, Lord, I want you too," she responded.

"I want you to walk close to Me."

"Yes, Lord, I want to walk close to You," she said.

Debbie practically ran to the front of the auditorium when someone invited those needing prayer to come forward. There a counselor met her and helped her as she prayed, confessing her sins to God and asking Jesus to be her personal Lord.

Ten months later she went to Jerusalem with her husband. One evening, as others gathered about him to pray, he too asked Jesus to be his Lord. Debbie was off to the side watching when she suddenly heard God's voice again: *"You and your husband will have a worldwide ministry."* At the time it sounded impossible since her husband was in the military and she was a stay-at-home mother.

That was twenty years ago. But in God's timing it came to pass. For the past seven years Debbie and her husband, who has now retired, have traveled to many nations reaching the unreached and ministering to pastors and leaders, some in undeveloped nations. It took time before God's word to her was fulfilled, but when it was it far exceeded what she could have dreamed.

God Gave Him Secrets in His Laboratory

George Washington Carver, the son of slaves who revolutionized agriculture, asked God for wisdom. He prayed, "Mr. Creator, show me the secrets of Your universe."

He said God told him, *"Little man, you are not big enough to know the secrets of My universe, but I will show you the secret of the peanut."* With that one secret, he made more than two hundred different products from the peanut. The knowledge of God about the peanut was enough to revolutionize the agriculture of the entire South and possibly the world.[4]

He called his laboratory at Tuskegee, Alabama, "God's Little Workshop," and as he prayed, great discoveries came to him. Dr. Carver advocated the diversification of crops, promoted peanut production, and was a pioneer in the field of plastics. He was honored as one of America's most influential and innovative agronomists.[5]

Since God is no respecter of persons He can speak to you and me anytime, anyplace, anyway—if we but listen.

My Promise Shell

I remember clearly a day the Lord spoke to me about my teenage son Keith as I walked the beach. Deeply concerned about his spiritual condition, I had watched helplessly as he seemed to drift further and further from the Lord. My only recourse was prayer. I realized that, as a parent, I had made many mistakes. So I asked the Lord to forgive me.

That late afternoon as I walked alone along the Atlantic I proclaimed aloud Scriptures tucked away in my heart. "The seed of the righteous shall be delivered," I shouted into the wind. "Because of Jesus' blood I am righteous and my children are my seed and they shall be delivered," I paraphrased. "All my children shall be taught of the Lord, and great will be their peace," I paraphrased again. (See Proverbs 11:21; Isaiah 54:13, KJV.)

Over and over I repeated scriptural promises God had given me for my children. I desperately needed an answer for my son. After more than an hour of this, I reached down and picked up a small brown and white shell that was being tossed about helplessly by the waves. When I did I had an inner witness that God was saying, *"Leave your fear here on the beach. Think about this shell. It had much potential for growth. So does your son. Just trust Me to polish and perfect him."*

I took my promise shell home, washed it in bleach, and set it on the kitchen window ledge. Often I'd pick it up, hold it high in the air, and say aloud, "Lord, You promised." Even when I saw no signs of change, I'd thank God for His word that He and He alone would perfect him.

It was a five-year battle in prayer. But one night when he called to ask his father and me to forgive him—and we asked him to forgive us too—he started his pilgrimage back to the

Lord. After college and a short career in graphic arts, he enrolled in a Bible school.

Recently he finished seven years with the Youth With A Mission organization. He's been twice to West Africa and to Indonesia, Thailand, and parts of Europe as a short-term missionary. He's taught communication skills to staff onboard the hospital ship *Anastasia,* and he's had the privilege of training others to go to the nations for Jesus while teaching at the University of the Nations in Hawaii.

Today he's a godly husband and father of two daughters. My "promise shell" still sits on my kitchen window, testimony to a prayer answer God gave me so many years ago.

Pastor Hears God With Intensity

Listen to the incredible encounter with God of an American pastor, Mike Bickle.

In Cairo, Egypt, in a little hotel, primitive by Western standards, Mike was interceding for the future church he'd start soon back in Kansas. He'd been kneeling on the cement floor by a rickety bed for almost thirty minutes when he heard from God. He didn't see a vision. He simply heard God speak to him. He writes of it:

It wasn't what some people call the audible voice. I call it the internal audible voice. I heard it as clearly as I would have heard it with my physical ears, and honestly, it was terrifying. It came with such a feeling of cleanness, power and authority. In some ways I felt I was being crushed by it. I wanted to leave, but I didn't want to leave. I wanted it to be over, but I didn't want it to be over. I only heard a few sentences, and it took just a few moments, but every word had great meaning. The awe of God flooded my soul as I experienced a little bit of the terror of the Lord. I literally trembled and wept as God Himself communicated to me in a way I've never known before or since.

The Lord simply said, "I will change the understanding and expression of Christianity in the earth in one generation."[6]

The pastor had further insight into the meaning of the message he received, but what struck me was his additional description: "My experience only lasted about thirty to sixty minutes, though it seemed like a couple of hours.... The awe of God lingered in my soul for hours. I woke up the next day still feeling its impact."[7]

God doesn't just whisper, as some would have us believe. He can speak any way He wishes. In the words of the Book of Job: "God's voice thunders in marvelous ways; He does great things beyond our understanding" (37:5).

One day as I drove to church a new billboard caught my attention, high up and near a topless bar. "Have You Heard Me?" The question in large black letters glared down at me. Below was a small photo of a new radio talk show host.

I thought to myself, *What if God's name was featured in the box instead of the face of a man? What if everyone who passed heard God ask if they had heard Him?* Can't you just imagine the various reactions? Drivers going to work. Students walking to the nearby school. Men entering the adult show.

God is speaking. Have we heard Him? We are learning, Lord.

Listening With Expectation

Joan of Arc put herself in a position to hear God's voice. In George Bernard Shaw's play *Saint Joan,* the king is annoyed because she hears from God but he doesn't. He asks, "Why don't your voices come to me? I am the king, not you."

She replies, "They do come, but you do not hear them. You have not sat in the field in the evening listening for them. When the angelus rings you cross yourself and have done with it. But if you prayed from your heart and listened to the thrilling of the bells in the air after they stopped ringing, you would hear as well as I do."[8]

Philip Yancey recalls an interview that broadcaster Dan Rather did with Mother Teresa of Calcutta. "What do you say to God when you pray?" he asked. Mother Teresa looked at him with her dark, soulful eyes and said quietly, "I listen." Slightly flustered, Rather tried again. "Well, then, what does God say?" Mother Teresa smiled. "He listens."[9]

We long for God to speak to us, to answer our prayers, to touch our lives, and to give us His guidance, protection, and direction. Yet He wants even more to talk with us—not just in our little daily devotional times, but any time, anywhere.

May we be as childlike as little Samuel, always open to say, "Speak, Lord, for your servant is listening!"

Wait expectantly, anxiously anticipating His voice!

Prayer

Lord, how often we confine You to a box of our own thinking, anticipation, and expectation. This day we choose to free You to speak to us at any time and in any way. Thank You that You will.

PART 12

A Final Word on the Word

ço

Throughout this book we have looked at the many ways God has spoken to people. Although our examination has included examples from the Bible, let's take a more extended tour of how the Word of God has recorded the words of God.

The Bible uses the words *hear, hearing, listen,* and *listening* more than eight hundred times. Among them are accounts of how and when God spoke to individuals.

The Consequences of Not Listening

In the Old Testament we read a sad account of God's people no longer wanting to hear His voice. At the foot of Mount Sinai He had made His voice known to them very specifically. Later, Moses tells us about their fateful decision:

> "Out of heaven He let you hear His voice, that He might instruct you; on earth He showed you His great fire, and you heard His words out of the midst of the fire....
>
> "The Lord talked with you face to face on the mountain from the midst of the fire.

"I stood between the Lord and you at that time, to declare to you the word of the Lord; for you were afraid because of the fire, and you did not go up to the mountain...."

DEUTERONOMY 4:36; 5:4,5 NKJV

The leaders confessed to Moses that they had heard His voice. Yet they expressed fear and unbelief, implying they didn't want to hear God directly but would listen to Him through His servant Moses. God told Moses to tell them to return to their tents. In other words, they could go on about their own business: "But as for you [Moses], stand here by Me, and I will speak to you all the commandments, the statutes, and the judgments which you shall teach them, that they may observe them in the land which I am giving them to possess..." (Dt 5:31, NKJV).

These Israelites never made it into the Promised Land, but their offspring did. It seems they chose to reject intimate conversation with God, depending instead on their leader Moses to hear God and give them His words. It was the last time God spoke in an audible voice to the people as a whole.

Prophets and Priests

After Moses, God used prophets and priests to speak for Him to His people. Then came Jesus. He taught His followers for three years, then He promised when He went away the Holy Spirit would come and teach them. Let's consider a few others from the Old Testament whom God used.

Jonah. When the word of the Lord came to Jonah with instructions to go to Nineveh and cry against its wickedness, he fled from the presence of the Lord. However, following his turbulent boat ride and subsequent entombment in the belly of the big fish, when the word of the Lord came a second time, he promised to obey. Now Jonah gladly went to Nineveh to deliver God's message. As a result the entire city fasted, repented, and was saved from destruction. (See Jonah 1:1-2; 3:1-2.)

Ezekiel. The prophet Ezekiel was told by God that he was a watchman over Israel—a spokesman for Him. He was instructed to "so hear the word I speak and give them warning from me" (Ez 33:7).

Samuel. At a time when the word of the Lord was rare and there were not many visions, God chose a young boy named Samuel as His mouthpiece. One evening, while he was sleeping in the temple, Samuel heard the Lord call his name three times before he replied, "Speak, Lord, for your servant is listening." What a hard message God gave him to deliver to his mentor, the priest Eli. It was a prophetic warning that his household was going to suffer for their sin. The Bible indicates the word came also with a vision. (See 1 Samuel 3:1-17.)

Jeremiah. It was written of Jeremiah, appointed by God as prophet to the nations, that the Lord Himself reached out His hand and touched his mouth, putting words in his mouth to speak. Jeremiah was on various occasions told where to stand to give God's messages. Once he was to stand at the gates of Jerusalem (Jer 17:19); yet another time he was to go to the potter's house to receive God's message (Jer 18:1-12).

Deborah. The prophetess Deborah had a word from God how to fight the battle against Jabin, king of Canaan, and his army commander, Sisera, who had nine hundred iron chariots. The

Israelites had been cruelly oppressed by them for twenty years. Deborah accompanied Barak to battle, and a woman named Jael killed Sisera when he sought comfort in her tent. (See Judges 4.)

Esther. Queen Esther took the advice of her cousin Mordecai, who had raised her, in how to approach the king. Her actions saved her people. But she listened and obeyed the direction of another. (See the book of Esther.)

Isaiah. The prophet Isaiah saw the Lord, "sitting on a throne, high and lifted up, and the train of His robe filled the temple." He said, "Woe is me, for I am undone! Because I *am* a man of unclean lips, And I dwell in the midst of a people of unclean lips; For my eyes have seen the King, The Lord of hosts." Then a seraphim took a live coal from the altar and touched his mouth and told him his iniquity was taken away and his sin purged. Then when the Lord said, "Whom shall I send?" Isaiah answered, "Here *am* I! Send me." (See Isaiah 6:1, 5-8, NKJV.) Isaiah essentially said, "Let me have the privilege of speaking for You with my lips!"

God Sometimes Sent Angels

God spoke directly to some people in the Bible. On other occasions He sent an angel, as recorded in both the Old and New Testaments.

Gideon was a young man beating out wheat in a winepress, essentially hiding from the Midianites, who had oppressed his people for seven years. He didn't want them to get his food. An angel appeared and said to him, "The Lord is with you, O valiant warrior." Now he didn't know for sure what to think of this message. His family, he argued, was the least in their tribe and he was the youngest member of his family.

He certainly didn't feel like a valiant warrior. When God's messenger told him he was to be the one to defeat Midian he had a lot of questions:

Why has this happened to my people, if the Lord is with us?

Will you give me a sign that it is God who is with me?

Where are the signs and wonders our fathers told us about?

We know God used him and a small army of three hundred to defeat a multitude of Midianites later, proving he was a mighty warrior. But we see a lesson in the life of Gideon: it is good to ask God questions. He learned that his people, the Israelites, had been disobedient to God.

God asked him first to tear down the altar of Baal that belonged to his father and to cut down Asherah that was beside it. (See Judges 6:11-7:25.) God may ask us to get rid of idols in our life too. We don't have any? Do we have anything that has preeminence in our life above God? A misplaced allegiance?

While ministering in the temple, the priest Zechariah (sometimes called Zacharias) encountered an angel, who told him his wife, Elizabeth, would bear a child, even in her old age. (See Luke 1:11-22.)

An angel appeared to the Virgin Mary, giving her the most cherished news a young Jewish virgin could expect (see Luke 1:26-38). An angel also came to her fiancé, Joseph, in a dream, telling him not to be afraid to take Mary as his wife, for the baby in her womb was of the Holy Spirit and His name was to be called Jesus, since He would save people from their sins. (See Matthew 1:18-24.)

An angel of the Lord spoke to the shepherds keeping watch over their sheep outside Bethlehem. They went to greet the baby Jesus, and a host of angels joined the first angel to herald the Savior's birth. (See Luke 2:8-20.)

An angel spoke to Philip, in the midst of his successful meetings, to travel south on the road from Jerusalem to Gaza. Unsure why, he just went. There traveling in a chariot was a court official of the queen of Ethiopia, reading the prophet Isaiah. The Holy Spirit instructed Philip to join his chariot. It soon became apparent why. He was able to explain to the eunuch that Jesus was the Messiah—the one foretold in Isaiah—and the man not only believed, he asked Philip to baptize him as a new convert. Scholars believe he returned to his land as a fervent missionary.

Notice that Philip received his first instructions from an angel and his second from the Spirit of God (see Acts 8:26-40). The apostle Peter, languishing in jail awaiting Herod's executioners, was suddenly surprised by an angel who led him out of prison. Escaping to the house of John Mark's mother, he found believers still praying for him. (See Acts 12:1-19.)

God Spoke Very Plainly

The conversion of Saul to Paul on his way to Damascus is as dramatic an account of hearing God's voice as one can imagine. Saul was en route to arrest Christians and take them as prisoners back to Jerusalem when a light from heaven flashed around him. Then the thundering voice of the Lord spoke directly to him—even the men traveling with him heard the voice—but they saw no one.

"Saul, Saul, why do you persecute me?"

"Who are you, Lord?" Saul asked.

"I am Jesus, whom you are persecuting," he replied. "Now

get up and go into the city, and you will be told what you must do" (Acts 9:4-6).

Saul got up, but when he opened his eyes, he couldn't see anything. He was blind. His friends led him to Damascus. For three days he neither ate or drank.

In that city, another man, Ananias, heard from God through a vision. The Lord gave him explicit instructions to go to the house of Judas and ask for a man from Tarsus named Saul. He was to lay hands on him so he would regain his sight. Ananias was frightened because he had heard of this ruthless persecutor of the Christians. But he obeyed. Paul became not only a Christian convert but a missionary who wrote many helpful instructions in what is now our New Testament to help us walk out our Christian faith. (See Acts 9.)

Paul later spoke more of what the Lord told him on the road to Damascus:

> "I have appeared to you to appoint you as a servant and as a witness of what you have seen of me and what I will show you. I will rescue you from your own people and from the Gentiles. I am sending you to open their eyes and turn them from darkness to light, and from the power of Satan to God, so that they may receive forgiveness of sins and a place among those who are sanctified by faith in me."
>
> ACTS 26:16-18

He Is Still Speaking

God is still speaking to us today, asking us to help bring people out of darkness into the light of the gospel of Jesus Christ.

You may be enriched to do a study of the ways He spoke through the Bible, as we have only considered the highlights. God spoke to ordinary men and women, asking them to carry out His instructions. We don't even know some of their names, but God knows all their names. He knows our names too and He longs to speak to us, just as He did to them. Are you listening?

Notes

Part 1
How Does God Speak?

1. David Wilkerson, "What It Means to Walk in the Spirit," *Times Square Church Pulpit Series,* August 15, 1994, 4.
2. Jn 16:13; Acts 9:31; 10:19; Mt 10:19-20; Rom 5:5; 8:26-27.
3. Mark Virkler, quoted in *Touching the Heart of God,* ed. Leonard LeSourd (Old Tappan, N.J.: Chosen, 1990), 59–60.
4. Quin Sherrer and Ruthanne Garlock, *A Woman's Guide to Spiritual Warfare* (Ann Arbor, Mich.: Servant, 1991), 201.
5. Elizabeth Alves, *The Mighty Warrior* (Bulverde, Tex.: Intercessors International, 1987), 69, 70.
6. Alves, 74–75.
7. Quin Sherrer and Ruthanne Garlock, *A Woman's Guide to Getting Through Tough Times* (Ann Arbor, Mich.: Servant, 1998), 114–15.
8. Peter Lord, *Hearing God* (Grand Rapids, Mich.: Baker, 1988), 27.

Part 2
His Voice at Life's Crossroads

1. Gordon T. Smith, *Listening to God in Times of Choice* (Downers Grove, Ill.: InterVarsity Press, 1997), 107.
2. Adapted from Sherrer and Garlock, *A Woman's Guide to Getting Through Tough Times,* 30–31.
3. Smith, 129.
4. Sherrer and Garlock, *A Woman's Guide to Getting Through Tough Times,* 129, 130.

Part 3
When God Says, "Let Go"

1. Fuchsia Pickett, *Receiving Divine Revelation* (Lake Mary, Fla.: Creation House, Strang Communications, 1997), 15.

Part 4
God Speaks to Us About Money

1. Benjamin Franklin, quoted in *Topical Encyclopedia of Living Quotations,* ed. Sherwood Eliot Wirt and Kersten Beckstrom (Minneapolis: Bethany House, 1982), 158.

2. Sherrer and Garlock, *A Woman's Guide to Spiritual Warfare,* 74–75.
3. Quin Sherrer and Ruthanne Garlock, *A Woman's Guide To Spirit-Filled Living* (Ann Arbor, Mich.: Servant, 1996), 191–92.
4. Wilkerson, 1.

Part 5
When God Tells Us to Pray

1. E.M. Bounds, quoted in *Topical Encyclopedia of Living Quotations,* 181.
2. Adapted from John and Paula Sandford, *Healing the Wounded Spirit* (Plainfield, N.J.: Bridge, 1982), 284. Used by permission of John Sandford.
3. Adapted from a transcript of a speech given by Leonard Crimp at a Men's Fellowship Meeting, Elora/Fergus, Canada, on September 29, 1990. Used with permission of family members.

Part 6
His Assurance in Difficult Times

1. Hannah Whitall Smith, *The God of All Comfort* (Chicago: Moody, 1956), 241.
2. John Hagee, ed., *Prophecy Study Bible, New King James Version* (Nashville, Tenn.: Thomas Nelson), 716.

Part 7
God Prepares Us for Life's Losses

1. Philip Yancey, *Finding God in Unexpected Places* (Ann Arbor, Mich.: Servant, 1997), 12.

Part 8
God Speaks Protection Over Our Lives

1. Betsie ten Boom, quoted in *Topical Encyclopedia of Living Quotations,* 93.
2. Paula Shields, as told to Quin Sherrer, *Miracles Happen When You Pray* (Grand Rapids, Mich.: Zondervan, 1997), 142–44. Used with permission.
3. Adapted from Sherrer and Garlock, *A Woman's Guide To Spiritual Warfare,* 58; Barbara Wentroble, *Wentroble Christian Ministries Newsletter* (October 1998), 1.
4. Adapted from Sherrer, *Miracles Happen When You Pray,* 103–5.

Part 9
Extraordinary Measures

1. Judith Couchman, *His Gentle Voice* (Sisters, Ore.: Multnomah, 1998), 126.
2. Cindy Jacobs, *The Voice of God* (Ventura, Calif.: Regal, 1995), 210.
3. Ann Spangler, *Dreams* (Grand Rapids, Mich.: Zondervan, 1997), 17.
4. Jacobs, 211.
5. Jack W. Hayford, Kingdom Dynamics footnotes in Spirit-Filled Life Bible (NKJV), Thomas Nelson Publishers, 1991, 1932.
6. Jacobs, 219.
7. Jacobs, 219.
8. Quin Sherrer and Ruthanne Garlock, *How to Pray for Your Family and Friends* (Ann Arbor, Mich.: Servant, 1990), 74–75.
9. Billy Graham, *Angels: God's Secret Agents* (Dallas: Word, 1986), 20.

Part 10
God Speaks His Love Through Others

1. Traci Mullins and Ann Spangler, *Vitamins for Your Soul* (New York: Doubleday, 1997), 81.
2. Dutch Sheets, *Intercessory Prayer* (Ventura, Calif.: Regal, 1996), 45.
3. Excerpted from an article, "The Chess Game," by Quin Sherrer, *Christian Life Magazine* (November 1982); used by permission of Strang Communications, Lake Mary, Florida.
4. Jack Hayford, *Pursuing the Will of God* (Sisters, Ore.: Multnomah, 1997), 127.

Part 11
Listening for God Anytime, Anywhere, Anyhow!

1. Hayford, *Pursuing the Will of God*, 117, 12.
2. Tommi Femrite, "Insights," *Intercessors International Magazine* (July 1998), 8. Used with permission.
3. Ann Landers, Life Section, *Colorado Springs Gazette*, August 16, 1998, 10.
4. Dr. Pat Robertson, adapted from a message given at Dallas Christ for the Nations, Summer 1998. Published in *Christ for the Nations Magazine* (September 1998), 6.
5. *Webster's New World Encyclopedia*, college edition (New York: Prentice-Hall, 1993), 200.

6. Mike Bickle, *Growing in the Prophetic* (Orlando, Fla.: Creation House, Strang Communications, 1996), 29–30. Used with permission.

7. Bickle, 31.

8. William Barclay, *The Gospel of Luke* (Philadelphia: Westminster, 1953), 5.

9. Yancey, 210.